# *Dreams of* DUNELAND

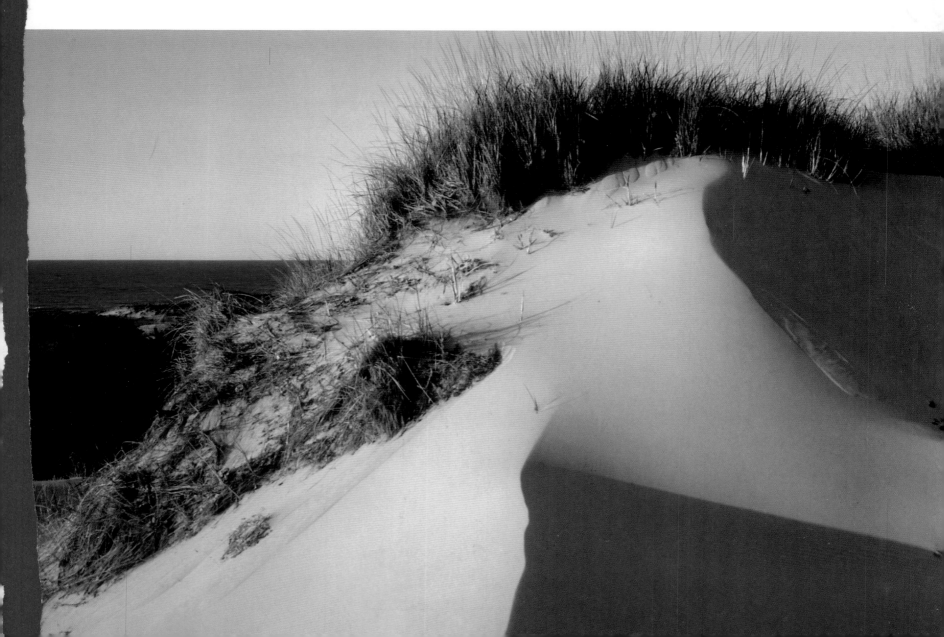

# Dreams of
# DUNELAND

*A Pictorial History of the Indiana Dunes Region*

## Kenneth J. Schoon

QUARRY BOOKS     *an imprint of*   INDIANA UNIVERSITY PRESS   BLOOMINGTON AND INDIANAPOLIS

*This book is a publication of*

Quarry Books
an imprint of

Indiana University Press
Office of Scholarly Publishing
Herman B Wells Library—350
1320 E. 10th Street
Bloomington, Indiana
47405 USA

iupress.indiana.edu

*Telephone orders*   800-842-6796
*Fax orders*   812-855-7931

♾ The paper used in this publication meets
the minimum requirements of the American
National Standard for Information Sciences-
Permanence of Paper for Printed Library
Materials, ANSI Z39.48-1992.

*Manufactured in China*

Library of Congress Cataloging-in-
Publication Data

Schoon, Kenneth J.
  Dreams of duneland : a pictorial history
of the Indiana Dunes Region / Kenneth J.
Schoon.
      p. cm.
  Includes bibliographical references and index.
  ISBN 978-0-253-00789-6 (cl : alk. paper)
— ISBN 978-0-253-00798-8 (eb)  1.  Indiana
Dunes State Park (Ind.)—History—Pictorial
works. 2.  Indiana Dunes National Lakeshore
(Ind.)—History—Pictorial works.  I. Title.
  F532.I5S35 2013
  977.2'98—dc23

                                2012028989

1  2  3  4  5    18  17  16  15  14  13

The peak of a sand dune, with beach
grasses, Indiana Dunes National
Lakeshore. *(facing) Larry Lawhead*

High Dune Crest, West Beach.
*(page i) © David A. Larson,
Ogden Dunes, Indiana*

*It is a country for the dreamer and the poet,*
*who would cherish its secrets,*
*open enchanted locks,*
*and explore hidden vistas,*
*which the Spirit of the Dunes has kept*
*    for those who understand.*

—EARL H. REED, *The Dune Country,* 1916

# CONTENTS

# PART ONE
# Scenes of Duneland

# PART TWO
## Stories of Duneland

ParKids at the Bailly Homestead.
*National Park Service (NPS),
Edwin Alcox*

Unlike Chicago's Lake Michigan coast, with its world-renowned scenic lakefront parks, Indiana's coast is hard to see. No parkway winds its way along Indiana's shore, and no bicycling or hiking path provides a continuous view of the lake.

In more than thirty years with the National Park Service, I have been fortunate to work in more than a dozen parks in nine states. Assignments have taken me to dozens of other national parks, and my travels have included every state in the union. There are few areas in the country I can think of that bring the mixture of emotion, hopes, dreams, disappointments, and successes as the Lake Michigan coast of Indiana. It is a place of surprises and superlatives.

Once a place of rolling sand dunes, pristine rivers, wetlands teeming with wildlife, and the crystal-clear waters of an enormous lake, the area of Northwest Indiana has seen a variety of forces tugging to make the land conform to their individual visions. Today, this land shows the results of those struggles between industry and nature, homes and recreation, isolation and inclusion. Enormous steel, chemical, and power-producing factories stand shoulder-to-shoulder with a national park and a state park. Railroads and interstate highways connect the nation running through small towns and beach communities where privacy is valued. The greatest freshwater resource in the western hemisphere has been irreversibly altered by non-native aquatic species and is frequently a place for the disposal of human and industrial waste.

Constantine Dillon, Superintendent, Indiana Dunes National Lakeshore. *NPS*

Telling the story of such a conflicted landscape is a challenge, and no single book could do it all. In this book, Ken Schoon offers a comprehensive overview of all this history and takes the reader on a virtual tour of time and space across the Indiana Dunes region.

The transformation of the region, from a Potawatomi homeland to an industrial and urban landscape, is told through historical vignettes and the aspirations of individuals who saw this area as a place to match their dreams. In many ways, the history of the Indiana Dunes area is a microcosm of the land use conflicts that are the hallmarks of the late twentieth century, when people awoke to the changes we had wrought on our own environment. For most of human history, people have shaped the lands and waters to fit their needs. We were so impressed with our ability to make these changes that we rarely stopped to consider the wisdom of these changes. Why would we befoul the air we breathe and the water we drink? Have we created landscapes we feel proud to leave our children? Is it prudent to destroy one of the country's most ecologically diverse landscapes for the short-term benefit of commerce?

And what of preservation? Is the wise use of our resources the same as no use of our resources? Has the anti-development attitude of NIMBY (Not In My Back Yard) thinking given way to BANANA (Build Absolutely Nothing Anywhere Near Anybody)? Is preservation the natural enemy of development, or can they work together to create a livable landscape? As we move further into the twenty-first century, these questions and conflicts will continue to shape our communities and our lands.

The term "interpretation" in reference to national parks means the art of educating the public about the resources and history of the park in such a way as to have meaning for the individual learner. We say that through interpretation comes understanding. Through understanding comes appreciation. From appreciation comes preservation. The essence of this adage is that one cannot shortcut this process. You cannot force a visitor to appreciate directly through interpretation. Individuals form their opinions based upon the information available to them, and their understandings are shaped by their personal attributes. Ken offers the reader ample opportunity for interpretation and understanding. It is up to the reader to decide what he or she values in the Indiana Dunes and what role to take in determining the future of this unique area.

Whether you are a resident of the area, a visitor, or merely an interested reader, Ken's journey through the dunes will fascinate you. Through the photographs and stories you will see a land as it once was, as it is now, and, for some dreamers, as it never would become. Stories of the abundant bounty when Lake Michigan supported a thriving commercial fishing industry. Photos of the stunning landscape that once stood where steel mills stand today. Descriptions of the famed icons the Hoosier Slide and Cowles Bog. Each step in his telling of history invites the reader to take the same journey as those who came here to make their mark.

Today, we no longer have the vast expanses of dunes, woodlands, prairies, and wetlands that drove people to want a national park here in 1915. Much has been lost. What remains is worth preserving, but the landscape that inspired Stephen Mather to advocate for a Dunes National Park is gone. It was not some force of nature or cataclysm that brought these changes—all were a result of human action. Choices made these changes. And choices will determine the future of the Indiana Dunes.

Just what kind of place is the Indiana Dunes? A place for relaxation in a residential community like Beverly Shores or Dune Acres. A place for recreation along the sandy shore. A place for exercise on one of the many trails. A place of employment at a power plant, railroad, or mill. A site for painting and poetic inspiration. A location for scientific exploration and youth education. And a place for preserving one of the most ecologically diverse environments in the nation. Amazingly, it is all these things and more, all packed within a short forty-five miles of coastline.

But this is not just a history book. This book is a guide, a conductor, to take you on your own trip through the dunes. Walk a trail, take a drive, visit a site, and use this book as your companion to find history that was and opportunities that are. You will find there is more here than you might have imagined.

Perhaps Ken's title says it all: *Dreams of Duneland,* for the Indiana Dunes have long been the place of dreams. Dreams realized and dreams dashed. Whatever the future holds for Indiana's Duneland, you can be sure that it will reflect the decisions and actions of the people of the region.

*Constantine Dillon, Superintendent,*
*Indiana Dunes National Lakeshore*

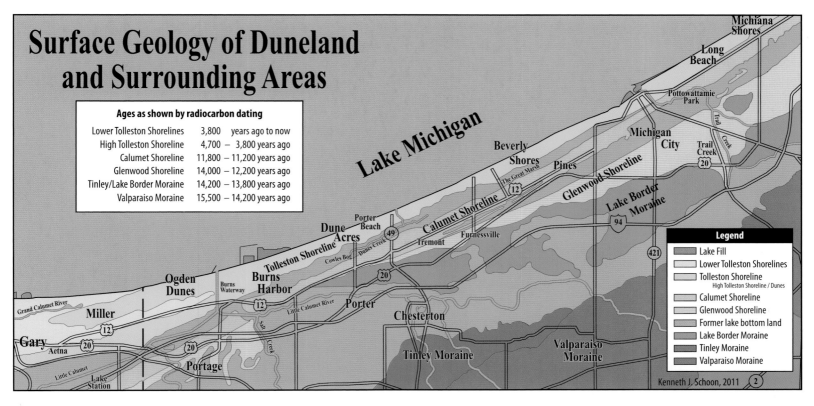

The surface geology of Duneland and surrounding areas.

*K. J. Schoon, 2012*

## Shorelines and Dunes

Generally speaking, within Duneland, the further the land is from the lakeshore, the older it is.

## The Glenwood Shoreline

Glacial Lake Michigan (formerly called Lake Chicago) was formed about 14,000 years ago when a glacier melted back from the Tinley/Lake Border Moraine and melt waters were trapped between the ice and the moraine. Of the three major ancient shorelines of Lake Michigan, the Glenwood is not only the oldest but also the highest (at 640 feet above sea level) and the farthest from the lake.

The first sand beach and the oldest sand dunes formed along this Glenwood Shoreline. Today they form a long band of low, forested hills generally between Highways 12 and 20 extending from Wagner Road northeast toward and beyond Greenwood Cemetery in Michigan City. Further west the shoreline is either buried by newer dunes or is south of the Duneland area.

Late in the Glenwood phase, about 12,200 years ago, the glacier retreated past the Straits of Mackinac, the lake level dropped dramatically, and the Glenwood phase was over.

## The Calumet Shoreline

A new shoreline formed about 11,800 years ago, when the glacier again advanced into the northern Lake Michigan basin and the lake basin slowly filled up again with rain and more glacial melt waters. When the lake level

*Duneland Dream. Pete Doherty, Doherty Images*

stabilized at about 620 feet above sea level, a new beach and series of sand dunes were formed, the Calumet Shoreline. This shoreline was a bit north of and twenty feet lower than the old Glenwood. Today this ancient beach can be found along Route 12 in eastern Porter County. In Michigan City, the Indiana State Prison and the International Friendship Gardens are on the Calumet Shoreline.

## The Tolleston Shorelines

The third of Lake Michigan's ancient shorelines is called the Tolleston Shoreline. The High Tolleston Shoreline got its start 4,700 years ago. It is north of and about fifteen feet lower than the Calumet Shoreline. As it formed, it was separated from the older Calumet Shoreline by a narrow band of lake water called the Calumet Lagoon. Roughly 3,800 years ago, the lake level starting dropping. The lagoon was separated from Lake Michigan, but it has largely remained a series of wetlands. Long Lake, Cowles Bog, Dunes Creek, and the Great Marsh are all remnants of this one-time part of Lake Michigan. The Tolleston Shoreline extends from these wetlands north to the lakeshore. It contains the tallest dunes in the area.

As the lake level continued to drop, it did so in a pulsating manner. The water level dropped because of erosion south of Lake Huron and rose during periods of greater rainfall. Toward the west, this rising and falling resulted in more than 150 small beach ridges between Miller and Chicago, all roughly parallel to the lakeshore. Geologist J. Harlan Bretz called these ridges the lower Tolleston beaches. Originally, they ranged in height from five to twelve feet and averaged about 150 feet in width. Although most of them were leveled as the industrial cities from Chicago to Gary were developed, a few can still be seen at Gibson Woods in Hammond, western Gary, and the Miller Woods section of the National Lakeshore.

## The Current Shoreline

It may come as a surprise to those who only occasionally make summer visits to the beach, but the current shoreline changes constantly. When the lake level is high, the beach is narrow. When the lake level is low, the beach is wider. With every wave, sand is brought up to the shore or washed away. In the dunes area, the overall current of the lake is from east to west, so sand that is washed into the lake often ends up back on the shore a bit further west.

Obstructions in the lake interrupt this flow and cause deposition of sand to the east of the obstruction and erosion to the west. Thus, shoreline erosion is an unwanted consequence of near-shore breakwaters and revetments. This has been called the single most destructive influence on the Indiana coast. It has caused the loss of beach, homes, roads, and dunes. The

*Star of Stones. Pete Doherty, Doherty Images*

effect is most easily seen at Michigan City harbor, which has been in place for more than 150 years, longer than any other obstruction.

## The Dunes

As hard as it might be to imagine, once upon a time there were no sand dunes along the Lake Michigan shoreline. As the last of the glacial ice receded from this area about 14,000 years ago, melt waters were trapped between the high glacial moraine to the south and the giant ice sheet to the north, and Lake Michigan (formerly called Lake Chicago) came into being. During this period of time, which is known as the Glenwood Phase, the ground was poorly drained, the shoreline was muddy and uneven, and the waters of the new Lake Michigan were icy cold. Almost immediately, wind and rain began to reshape what the glaciers had left behind.

As more ice melted, Lake Michigan grew. Blowing winds whipped up lake water into waves, which then began the now-familiar pattern of washing up on the shore. Riptides returned waters back to the lake. Then as now, each large wave moved some sand onto, along, or away from the beach. At the same time, lake currents moving southward along the eastern shore of Lake Michigan began moving sand toward the south shore of the lake. This action gave the South Shore area a huge amount of raw material for eventual dune building.

A two-step process thus created and is still altering the Indiana Dunes. Waves deposit sand upon the beach, and winds roll, bounce, or blow that sand inland, where it settles when the wind dies down. So in the same way that wind blows snow into drifts, it blows sand into dunes. Obstructions, such as driftwood or marram grass, can slow the wind. Marram grass thrives on the beach, even when it is buried by sand. A clump of marram grass can thus initiate and then sustain the process of dune formation. Farther inland, cottonwood trees also contribute to dune formation. Once these fast-growing and sand-tolerant pioneers establish themselves near the beach, they also slow the wind and thus become buried by sand. When they are buried, rather than dying as do many other trees, they send out new roots and keep growing upward.

Much has happened in the 14,000 years since Lake Michigan first appeared. The waters warmed. Fish and other aquatic species found their ways into the lake, and grasses and trees began to cover the land.

As the wind has not stopped blowing, so the dunes have not stopped changing. Just as a snowdrift can get larger during a snowy and windy winter night, so sand dunes can get larger over time. Dunes may also migrate. Wind may pick up sand from the windward side of a dune and blow it up and over to the other side. When this happens, the dune is called a "wandering dune." In a high wind, the sand blowing off the top of a wandering dune

The Lake Michigan shoreline from Beverly Shores to Michigan City. This photograph clearly shows where shoreline erosion has occurred west of the Michigan City harbor. *(facing) NPS, Constantine Dillon*

*Sandy Slope.*
*Pete Doherty,*
*Doherty Images*

can look like smoke. Smoking Dune at West Beach and Mouth Baldy west of Michigan City are wandering dunes. Mount Baldy moves about five feet downwind (southeast) every year. An advancing dune will bury whatever is on the leeward side of the dune: grass, trees, smaller dunes, a forest, perhaps even lost car keys. It is said that a derailed locomotive lies under one of the moving dunes west of Ogden Dunes. Plant growth, however, can stop this migration. As plant life is established on the dunes, their roots and fallen leaf mass begin to hold the sand in place. As the plants eventually multiply and cover the dune, the dune is stabilized.

Human activity causes changes in our dunes as well. Every time hikers climb a dune, their very footsteps push sand downward a little. On a larger scale, continued use by off-road vehicles can destroy the vegetation that had stabilized the dunes, resulting in resumed wind erosion.

Perhaps some of the most awesome sites in Dune Country are its blow-outs. On occasion, something can happen to remove the vegetation from a dune. This might be a man-made excavation or a natural change in lake level resulting in an excess amount of sand blowing inland. With the vegetative protection gone, strong winds can then pick up the exposed sand and blow it away. Over time, a blowout may be covered again with vegetation and thus again stabilized, or it may instead grow as more and more sand is blown away. Our largest amphitheater-shaped blowouts are larger than football fields.

A vital part of Dune Country are its wetlands. Interdunal ponds, great marshes, fens, and bogs can all be found in Duneland. Although generally peaceful in appearance, as opposed to the tall dunes and dynamic blow-outs, these natural bodies of water are also in a continual mode of change. Besides the annual variation in vegetation caused by the changing seasons, these wetlands are also affected by changes in the water table caused by periods of drought, heavy rains, or man-made excavations or pumping.

It was at the dunes that Henry Chandler Cowles was able to find landscapes of different ages (Glenwood/Calumet/Tolleston/Recent) right next to each other. He noted that the plant communities of these landscapes differed and thus was able to determine how plant communities at the dunes have changed over the years. His theory of plant succession was a result of his work. Another result of his work is that the Indiana Dunes are often referred to as the birthplace of ecology.

Change is a fascinating feature of Duneland. The glaciers of old, today's wind, rain, and waves, the seasons, animals, and people have all contributed to an endless changing landscape, the landscape of the Indiana Dunes.

ERRATA

Unfortunately, much local history material contains errors, and it would be presumptuous to assume that this book has eliminated them all and has no errors of its own. Readers are therefore encouraged to send corrections to the author at kschoon@iun.edu. Please be specific and, if possible, include some way that the author can confirm the correction. An updated list of errata will be available upon request.

A copy of the foot-noted manuscript is held at the Calumet Regional Archives, Indiana University Northwest, and is available for researchers. Please note that photographs have been taken by K. J. Schoon unless otherwise indicated.

After a 2.25 mile hike through various ecosystems, students from the Dunes Learning Center reach the top of a dune and see what might be Indiana's grandest view: Wooded foredunes, miles of beautiful beach, and a gorgeous lake. *Dunes Learning Center*

# ACKNOWLEDGMENTS

The author offers his sincere thanks to the following people who assisted with the writing of this book:

For suggesting that I begin this project, Susan MiHalo.

For finding facts, figures, and photos, IU Northwest Archivist Steve McShane; IU Northwest Instructional Media personnel Daniel Ichinose, Karen Newlin, Paul Sharpe, and Tome Trajkovski; librarians, curators, and researchers Larry Clark, David Hess, Eva Hopkins, David Kiehn, Carl O. Reed, Laura Shields, and Jane Walsh Brown; Anne Koehler, national and state park personnel Edwin Alcox, Brandt Baughman, Brad Bumgardner, Judy Collins, Christine Gerlach, Tricia Hodge, Marcus Key, Daniel Mason, Ruthanne Slamka, Wendy Smith, Kim Swift, and Superintendent Costa Dillon; industry representatives Erin DiPietro, Liz Folkerts, Nick Meyer, and Katie Patterson; graphic artist Jim Fields; also, Marilyn Arvidson, Peter Avis, Bruce Ayers, Nicole Kamins Barker and the staff at Save the Dunes, Nancy Jahnel Barnes, Lee Botts, Brian Breidert, Ken Brock, Jean Graham Buckley, Paul L. Childress, Spencer Cortwright, Erin Crofton, Bryan Dayson, Joyce Ebert Davis, Nancy Douglass, Janet Edwards, Dale Engquist, Clara Harmening, John Hayes, the late Ed Hedstrom, Gregg Hertzlieb, Steve Hornyak, Pamela James, Lewis Jones, Barbara Keinbaum, Matt Keiser, Zoran Kilibarda, Michael Kobe, Kris Krouse and the staff at Shirley Heinze Land Trust, Dani Lane, Ken Larson, Patrick Leacock, Johnny Martinez, Dick Meister, Susan MiHalo, Jason Miller, Mike Molnar, Zella Olson, Francis H. Parker, Noel Pavlovic, Trent Pendley, Raquel Perez, Jerry Peters, Marti Pizzini,

Dan Plath, Chief Boatswain's Mate Rebecca Polzin, Jude Rakowski, Herb and Charlotte Read, Mark Reshkin, Janice Rice, Steve Spicer, Mark Stanek, Michael Swygert, Todd Thompson, Lake County Surveyor George Van Til and supervisor Susan Harmening, Bill Warrick, the staff at Fort Ligonier, Bill Wild, Sandi Weindling, and Peter Youngman.

For allowing me to use their wonderful photographs and artwork: Diana Birky, Kermit Clyne, Peter Dougherty, Tom Dogan, Jim Fields, Michael Gant, Tony Gaul, M. A. Griswold, Lee Hibbs, Indiana Department of Natural Resources, Indiana Historical Society, Kira Kaufmann, Michael Kobe, David A. Larson, Rich Manalis, Christopher A. Meyers, Carol Moore, National Park service staff and volunteers, Zella Olson, Bj Parmley, Dan Plath, James Rettker, Jim Sprandel, Kim Swift, Ron Trigg, Bill Warrick, Gordon Wilder, Elaine Wojcinski, Carol Wood, Fredric Young, the Bauer Museum of Art, and Marikay Peter Witlock, for her superb paintings of the dunes and lakeshore.

For reviewing parts of the manuscript and making invaluable suggestions: Marilyn Arvidson, Brandt Baughman, Lee Botts, Brad Bumgardner, Costa Dillon, Dale Engquist, Jackie Glidden, Pamela James, Dani Lane, Jerry Peters, Carl O. Reed, Janice Rice, Steve Spicer, and Michael Swygert.

For finding books, articles, and miscellaneous information, for accompanying me on research trips, for copy editing, and for compiling the index, Peg Schoon.

The author and IU Press also thank Indiana University Northwest Academic Affairs, the Legacy Foundation, Friends of Indiana Dunes, and Save the Dunes for funds that allowed for the larger page size and the inclusion of so many color photographs.

Photographer Jim Rettker catches another photographer about to catch a beautiful Michigan City sunset. *Jim Rettker*

*Beachfront Trees.* Cottonwood trees are very adaptable to the shifting sands of the Indiana Dunes. *(left) Pete Doherty, Doherty Images*

Driftwood, Indiana Dunes National Lakeshore, Lake Michigan. *(overleaf) Steve Geer*

A foursome going down for a swim. *(overleaf) Ron Trigg*

Indiana University Northwest Academic Affairs

The Legacy Foundation

Friends of Indiana Dunes

Save the Dunes

# PART ONE
# Scenes of Duneland

Sap being cooked
in wooden bowls.
*(left) K. J. Schoon*

Stop 1. *(facing) NPS,
Jeff Manuszak*

# Maple Sugar Time

## March 5 & 6 and March 12 & 13
## 10 a.m. - 4 p.m.

Maple Sugar Time activities consist of an early spring walk through five demonstration stations in the Chellberg Farm area that demonstrate the enthusiasm for and making of maple syrup and maple sugar in Duneland over the centuries.

STOP 1 · The American Indian Sugar Camp. Indians poured sap into hollowed-out wooden bowls and then cooked it by placing hot rocks into the sap. If it is cooked long enough, it turns into sugar, always appreciated during and after a long, hard winter.

Sap drips from a spout into a collection bucket.

# DRAWN BACK BY THE TASTE OF MAPLE SUGAR

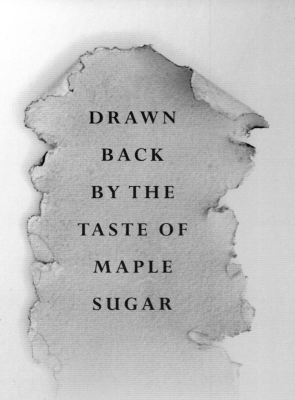

In the 1830s, Sagganee, a Potawatomi chief (perhaps the same person as Shabbona), went with the rest of his tribe to Kansas, but later returned, saying that he could not live in Kansas because there were no "sugar trees." He so enjoyed making maple sugar from the sap of sugar maples that he spent the rest of his life in Indiana, where sugar maples were plentiful.

STOP 2 · Visitors see how pioneers cooked down the sap in iron pots. *NPS, both images by Jeff Manuszak*

STOP 3 · Here visitors can practice drilling holes and hanging collecting buckets, as the Chellbergs did in the 1930s. *(left) NPS, Jeff Manuszak*

STOP 4 · The Sugar Shack. The Chellbergs' son-in-law Alden Studebaker built this sugar shack in the 1930s to be able to make and sell enough maple syrup and sugar to pay the family's taxes. *(below) NPS, Jeff Manuszak*

In the Sugar Shack. *NPS, Jeff Manuszak*

5

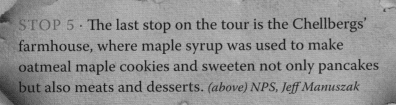

STOP 5 · The last stop on the tour is the Chellbergs' farmhouse, where maple syrup was used to make oatmeal maple cookies and sweeten not only pancakes but also meats and desserts. *(above) NPS, Jeff Manuszak*

*Above,* Ranger Kip Walton helps a young visitor with the maple syrup yoke, showing how folks carried two heavy buckets of syrup in the old days. *Below,* fresh-baked maple oatmeal cookies coming right out of the oven. *NPS, Jeff Manuszak*

The first green sprouts.
*Tom Dogan*

# Spring in Duneland

May apples emerge from beneath leaf clutter. *Ron Trigg*

Spring greenery. *(below) Ron Trigg*

Chellberg Farm yard in early spring. *Jim Rettker*

Charlotte and Herb Read on an April walk through the Cowles Bog area. *(above) Jon L. Hendricks for The Times of Northwest Indiana*

The two-story Bailly log cabin. *(facing) Michael Kobe*

## Green Dreams Awaken from a Cold, Dark Earth

In the longer days of March and April, with most weeks a bit warmer than the ones before, Duneland awakes from its winter sleep, and bits of green can be found along the forest floor.

At first unrecognizable, the plants soon develop leaves that aid in their identification, and the color of the woods and wetlands begins to change from brown to green.

*Soon the grass is green, but the trees are still bare . . .*

*. . . then the treetops begin to show a hint of green*

*Fair are the meadows,*
*Fairer still the woodlands*
*Robed in the blooming*
*garb of spring*

—17TH C. HYMN, ANON.

A deer path. *(left) Michael Kobe*

A foursome going down for a swim. *(above) Ron Trigg*

Spring at the Great Marsh. *(right) NPS, Kim Swift*

Lupines in bloom along the path between the Waverly Road trailhead and Howes Prairie. *(below) Jim Rettker*

*Wildflowers begin their annual awakening*

Marsh marigold.

Trillium.

Yellow trout lily.

Wild geranium.

Yellow lady's slipper.
*All photos by Ron Trigg*

Wild columbine.

*Finally the earth is alive in a sea of color*

Prickly pear cactus. *Ron Trigg*

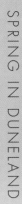

Prickly pear cactus grows in all of the deserts of the American southwest—and on the sandy soils throughout the Indiana Dunes. Their flat, fleshy pads look like green leaves but are actually modified stems that store water and support photosynthesis and flower production. They bloom in late spring. These cacti have sharp spines and are a good reminder that hikers should wear sturdy shoes and walk only on marked trails.

A hike under flowering dogwood. *(right) Dunes Learning Center*

# Summer

*By far, Duneland's most popular season*

*Dunes in Bloom. (above) Pete Doherty, Doherty Images*

Portage Lakefront and Riverwalk, the newest public
beach in Duneland. *Pete Doherty, Doherty Images*

Goat's rue.

Western sunflower.

## Summer blossoms · the color spectacular continues

Sullivant's milkweed. *(above)*

Compass Plant. *(left)*

*All photos by Ron Trigg*

New England aster.

Savanna blazing star.

Fringed gentian.

Stiff goldenrod.

# The Beach

Marram grass at Porter Beach.
*Ron Trigg*

Alex Rettker empties sand from his shoes. At the dunes, this is often the last activity of the day. *(below) Photo by his grand-father Jim Rettker*

*One of the best anywhere*

Digging for digging's sake. *(left) Dunes Learning Center*

*Glassy Shores. (above) Pete Doherty, Doherty Images*

Miller Beach, 1917. The bathing suits and the houses on shore could be rented from the Carr family. *(right) Calumet Regional Archives*

## Going to the Beach

People have been going to the beach to relax, to swim, and to get away from the daily grind for more than a hundred years. On hot summer days, the beach is cooler and breezier than the city. The water is refreshing. Before people owned their own bathing suits, they could rent them at the beach.

*Having fun on shore and surf*

The ever-popular beach at Dunes State Park. *(above)*
Playing in the surf. *(left) Dunes Learning Center*

Duneland beaches have often been recognized
as being among the best in the nation. They've
recently been recognized by *USA Today,*
*Midwest Living,* and *Parents Magazine.*

*Surfing—yes, it can be done on Lake Michigan!*

(From top to bottom)
Burying one's best friend: an ancient tradition on the beach. *Carol Moore*

Sand fort builders.
*Dunes Learning Center*

A sea creature and its creators.
*Dunes Learning Center*

Hobie cats line the beach at Ogden Dunes. *(top)*
Surfing on a homemade surfboard. *(above)*
*Photos by Lee Hibbs*

# The end of the day

A dip after volleyball. *Dunes Learning Center*

Sunset through marram grass. *Lee Hibbs*

Driftwood. *Lee Hibbs*

Dreamy Evenings

*The twilight comes,*
*the picture fades,*
*but the spell remains.*

—EARL H. REED,
*The Dune Country,* 1916

*Something magical about dusk and sunset at the dunes*

Evening campfires cast a
magical spell. *Carol Moore*

23

# Duneland Landscapes

Boardwalk. *Kermit Clyne*

*The dunes are to the Midwest what the Grand Canyon is to Arizona and Yosemite is to California. They constitute a signature of time and eternity: Once lost the loss would be irrevocable.*

—CARL SANDBURG IN A LETTER TO PAUL DOUGLAS, 1958

## The Sand Dunes

Along and near the shore of Lake Michigan are many dunes and dune-types. There are fore dunes, moving dunes, stable dunes, high dune ridges, and low dune and swale landscapes. The tallest dune is Mount Tom in the state park. The fastest moving dune is Mount Baldy in the National Lakeshore. The smallest dune? That might have formed yesterday near the beach—and tomorrow it may be gone with the wind.

High Dune Crest, West Beach. © *David A. Larson, Ogden Dunes, Indiana*

Central Beach dunes. *NPS, Jeff Manuszak*

Mount Baldy, November 26, 2008 *(above)* and again on November 29, 2010. *(right)*
*Photos by Zoran Kilibarda*

Indiana University Northwest geology professor Zoran Kilibarda has been studying the rate of motion of Mount Baldy and has discovered that it is moving faster than expected. (Use the concrete steps as a frame of reference to see how far the dune advanced in just two years.) The dune is the site of enormous future management and preservation problems. Its movement will soon result in the dune burying its own parking lot.

## Woodlands

Duneland woodlands are diverse. Here one can find old-growth and new-growth forests, black oak forests, and beech/maple forests. Woodlands are home to Duneland's largest mammal, the white-tailed deer. Trails through these woodlands provide wonderful experiences at any time of year.

*Cooler in the shade*

*Dunes Trail. Pete Doherty, Doherty Images*

27

*Part prairie, part woodland*

The savanna at Howes Prairie. *Jim Rettker*

## Savannas

A savanna is a grassland ecosystem with trees far enough apart that sunlight reaches the ground and a low, unbroken layer of herbaceous plans growing near the ground. It has some characteristics of both woodlands and prairies.

## Water and Wetlands

Bogs, fens, ponds, rivers, creeks, small lakes, and one "great" lake. Duneland has water. Wetlands are "in-between" areas: those areas that are saturated with water often enough to support vegetation adapted for life in saturated soils. Wetlands may have some pockets of shallow standing water, and they may be the most biologically diverse of all ecosystems. They are extremely important for filtering and cleaning water and helping to control flooding.

Miller Woods Lagoon. *NPS, Kim Swift*

*Nature's reservoirs and filters*

Naturalist and author Joel Greenberg notes that no type of landscape has undergone a greater change in the public's mind than wetlands. A century ago, wetlands were considered a nuisance, and draining them was called "reclaiming the land," a civilizing project. Today those wetlands that remain are somewhat protected. Although wetlands still disappear, at least many are replaced by the creation of wetlands elsewhere. Today in Duneland, there are many efforts to restore wetlands that were destroyed years back.

## Prairies

The dominant plants on prairies are grasses, herbs, and shrubs rather than trees.

The National Lakeshore has the seventh-greatest plant diversity of all US national parks because it has plants typical of prairies, wetlands, woodlands, and savannas—plus some plants typical of arctic regions and others native to the desert Southwest—all in one park.

The prairie at the John Merle Coulter Nature Preserve. *Ron Trigg*

*Sunny grasslands*

*A desert-like landscape surrounded by greenery*

Duneland blowout. *Michael Kobe*

## Blowouts

A blowout is an erosional feature produced by the wind. Blowouts occur when something removes the vegetation from a dune and the wind starts blowing the sand away. Blowouts can grow to sizes larger than a football field.

## Dune and Swale

Dune and swale topography is composed of dozens of parallel dune ridges, separated by long and narrow wet swales, and can be found from Miller westward around the lakeshore to south Chicago. The landscape was formed by the alternate lowering and rising levels of Lake Michigan over the last 4,500 years, each rise being a bit lower than the previous one.

It's easiest to see in winter, when leaves don't hide the view.

*Alternating elongated ridges and wetlands*

Miller Woods (look carefully for the parallel ridges). *NPS, Kim Swift*

# Duneland Fauna & Fungi

Red squirrel.

Chipmunk.

Raccoon. *M. A. Griswold, M.S.*

Gray squirrel.

White-tailed deer. *(above and below)*

Rabbit.

Springtime path. *(facing) Daniel Schwen*

*All photos by Ron Trigg except as noted*

*Four-footed friends in the forest*

## Mammals

There are at least 46 species of mammals found in Duneland, most of which are seldom seen by the casual visitor. However, if one is quiet and observant, several of the ones pictured here might make themselves known.

## Birds

According to Dr. Ken Brock, author of *Birds of the Indiana Dunes,* more than 350 species of birds have been seen in the dunes area. This large number is because of the north-south orientation of Lake Michigan, which provides a flight route for migrating species. Nineteen of those species are pictured on these pages.

Hawk. *(left) Tom Dogan*
Seagull. *(below left) Lee Hibbs*

Canada Geese. *Tom Dogan*

Mallards. *Michael Kobe*

Mute Swan. *Tom Dogan*

*On land, sea, and sky*

American Bald Eagle flying over the beach. *Tom Dogan*

Great Blue Heron. *NPS*

Wild Turkey. *Ron Trigg*

Great Egret. *Ron Trigg*

Blue Jay. *Tom Dogan*

Scarlet Tanager. *NPS*

Nuthatch. *Michael Kobe*

Redwing Blackbird. *Michael Kobe*

Red-bellied Woodpecker. *Tom Dogan*

Red-headed Woodpecker. *Tom Dogan*

Pileated Woodpecker. *Tom Dogan*

Sandhill Crane in flight. *(above) Michael Kobe*

Cardinal. *(right) Jim Rettker*

37

## Amphibians

Most amphibians are small animals. The bullfrog, up to eight inches long and weighing up to one pound, is one of the largest. The others are not only smaller, but quieter. Being cold-blooded, amphibians are only seen (or heard) when it's warm enough for them to be active. Only 18 species of amphibians are known to inhabit Duneland.

*Often declining globally, but hanging on locally*

Green frog.

Blue spotted salamanders.

Wood frog.

American toad.

Redback salamander.

*All photos by Ron Trigg*

## Reptiles

Twenty-three species of reptiles live in Duneland. Like amphibians, they are cold-blooded. Unlike amphibians, their skin is covered with scales. Both groups generally avoid human contact (as described by naturalist Joel Greenberg) "by clinging to the security of darkness or the safety of water."

Painted turtle

Garter snake (harmless to humans).

The endangered Blanding's turtle.

Box turtle. *All photos by Ron Trigg*

*Shy, cold-blooded residents*

39

# *Nature's artistry in miniature*

## Butterflies

Monarch on goldenrod.

Fritillary on common milkweed.

Tawny crescent.
*Michael Kobe*

American copper.

Painted lady.

Buckeye.
*Michael Kobe*

Tiger swallowtail on blazing star. *All photos by Ron Trigg except as noted*

Skipper (and a lady bug).

Sulfur.

Viceroy.

Black swallowtail *(left)* and Monarch caterpillar. *(above)*

*All photos by Michael Kobe*

# Endangered but doing better

Karner blue on butterfly weed. *NPS, Randy Knutson*

## The Karner Blue Butterfly

Duneland is home to the Karner blue butterfly, a small blue-and-gray butterfly that is on the federal list of endangered animals. This butterfly is a native of the Great Lakes region but is at risk because nearby land development and long-term fire suppression have resulted in habitat loss.

The caterpillars of the Karner blue feed solely on the leaves of wild lupine plants that grow in the partially sunny savannas near the lakeshore. As fires are suppressed, trees and other woody species gradually encroach on savannas, suppressing the lupine plants. Indiana Dunes staff, environmental groups, volunteers, and even local businesses have restored oak savanna habitats by creating and enlarging canopy openings and reducing woody undergrowth. Park staff also conducts careful prescribed burns to create or preserve habitat areas.

Lupine at West Beach. *(left) Kim Swift*
Karner blue on a pink tablecloth. *(below) NPS*

Bumblebee on a thistle. *(top right)*
Longhorned grass-hopper. *(middle right)*
Wasp on goldenrod. *(bottom right)*
*All photos by Michael Kobe*

*Other*

*photogenic*

*insects*

Widdow skimmer. *(top left)*
Twelve spotted skimmer dragonfly and
Ruby meadowhawk. *(middle left)*
Katydid. *(bottom left)*
*All photos above by Ron Trigg*

## Fungi

Fungi are often unnoticed until they develop their fruiting bodies. Then they can become quite photogenic. Fungi perform an essential role in nature in the decomposition of organic matter. Some are used as food, but many are poisonous. According to Indiana University Northwest professor Peter Avis, the National Lakeshore has one of the best-known forest fungal communities in any national park. Many of these fungi are notably different from those of similar forests, making this site even more important for research. Duneland has more than six hundred different species of fungi. This is a small sample of the more photogenic ones. *(All photos by Ron Trigg)*

Coral fungus *(above)* and Sulfur shelf. *(below)*

Turkeytail. *(below)*

Dryad's saddle.

*More than just mushrooms*

Shelf fungus. *(above)*

Earthstar. *(right)*

45

## More Fungi

*All photos by Ron Trigg*

Tree fungus.

Tuningfork.

Parasol.

Deathangel.

Dreaming of an easy dinner
at the Dunes State Park
Nature Center. *Jim Rettker*

# Summer Activities

Raising a May Pole starts the festivities (in spite of its being June).

*How Swedes celebrate the first day of summer*

There is much to do all across Duneland, from Miller Beach to Michigan City. Organized programs begin with the Midsummer programs near the summer solstice and continue to the end of summer in September. Every month has something special. Activities range from quiet canoe or kayak trips down scenic rivers to exciting air and boat shows.

Of course, the beaches and trails are available every day, and the campgrounds are available for those who want to spend the night in the middle of it all.

## Midsummer

Midsummer is a Scandinavian holiday. The short summer is especially appreciated, and so its first day (the longest day of the year) is a happy one.

The Chellbergs and their neighbors celebrated their Swedish heritage every year. Friends and descendants of Swedes, the largest ethnic group in the Chesterton-Miller area in the early days, keep the old traditions going.

*Nordikids* sing traditional Scandinavian songs at the Midsummer Festival at the Chellberg Farm.

Children had Swedish games to play.

Lingonberry Jam entertains with lively traditional music. *(above)*

Dans Norden, traditional Scandinavian folk dancers from Indianapolis, entertain the crowd. *(lower right)*

*All photos by NPS, John Roquet*

July at Indiana Dunes State Park

## Sand Sculpture Contest

The first Sand Sculpture Contest at Indiana Dunes State Park was held in 1998. Since then, it has become a highly anticipated event drawing contestants from across the state. With the exception of food coloring, participants may use only natural materials that they find on the beach. First-timers soon discover that sand dries out quickly and that a spray bottle comes in handy to keep the sand firm and moist.

A small sample of the 2011 sculptures is shown here.

The *J. D. Marshall* (a ship that sank in Lake Michigan in 1911). *(facing)*

A Mayan pyramid. *(left)*

The space shuttle (which was then on its last flight).

51

A butterfly.

Prizes each year are provided by Friends of Indiana Dunes.

The Washington Monument and reflecting pool. *(above)*
The Pirates of the Caribbean. *(left)*

A hand, arm, and bracelet (made of beach stones).

The beach at Marquette Park during the Air Show. *Frederic Young*

## Gary's South Shore Air Show

Since 2000, American's most exciting aircraft have returned to aviation's birthplace for Gary's annual South Shore Air Show. Admission and shuttle service are free, with a charge only for parking. Friday night before the show features a "twilight show" with all the acts from the actual shows on Saturday and Sunday, topped off with fireworks. Beside activity in the air, there are food and souvenir vendors, a kids zone, a beer garden, and interactive military displays in the park.

The mid-July Air Show is the biggest annual event in Northwest Indiana, drawing an estimated 600,000 people every year to Gary's Marquette Park and surrounding areas. It's the only three-day show in the Chicago area, and the planes and aviators provide an outstanding show. Many of them return to Gary in August, as the Gary airport is the staging area for Chicago's air show.

Pictured here are the United States Air Force's Thunderbirds and the stealth bomber. Note the number 5 on the plane flying upside down. It is painted upside down so that it appears right side up in flight. *Photos by Tom Dogan*

*Racing some of the fastest boats on earth*

### Great Lakes Grand Prix

The Great Lakes Grand Prix is part of the Super Boat International offshore powerboat summer racing schedule and features many of the world's fastest and most powerful boats speeding past spectators at speeds close to 150 miles per hour.

The first annual Great Lakes Grand Prix was held off the Washington Park beach in August of 2009. It attracted the best North American competitors and thousands of spectators, who watched both from the shore and from hundreds of pleasure boats in the lake.

*Logo by Jim Fields. Photos by Tom Dogan*

Michigan City mayor Chuck Oberlie pilots what might be the strangest vessel ever to ply the waters off the Duneland coast, the Lake Erie Marine Trades Association's "Hot Dog Boat," built for the 1976 San Francisco Sports and Boat Show. *Lake Erie Marine Trades Association*

The crowded piers at the Michigan City In-Water Boat Show. *Lake Erie Marine Trades Association*

## Michigan City In-Water Boat Show

The first annual Michigan City In-Water Boat Show was held at Michigan City's Washington Park in 1980, with sixty manufacturers, distributors, and dealers from the Lake Michigan area participating. Since then it has become the largest in-water boat show on Lake Michigan and one of the largest and longest-running boat shows on the Great Lakes. The show runs each year for four days during the last week of August.

Boat lovers need not just dream about their new boat; they can board, compare, and purchase their new or "pre-owned" boats and accessories right in town. The show also features boating safety presentations and entertainment. The Lake Erie Marine Trades Association that runs the show keeps returning to Northwest Indiana because of Michigan City's great harbor facilities and nearby expressways.

## Shipwrecks and Scuba Diving

Sad reminders of Indiana's maritime history are the many ships lying today on the bottom of the lake. Some, like the *Muskegon,* were deliberately scuttled. Others, such as the *J. D. Marshall,* which in 1911 sank near where Dunes State Park is today, were the victims of storms and sank, causing loss of life.

There are hundreds of shipwrecks in the lake, many dozens in Indiana waters and perhaps most near the Michigan City harbor. Only fourteen, however, have been located. Historic shipwrecks provide information about past nautical technology and commerce. To save historic shipwrecks from harm, Congress in 1987 passed the *Abandoned Shipwrecks Act,* which gave title of historic shipwrecks to the states. Indiana's Department of Natural Resources now protects these shipwrecks from looters and salvagers.

The known shipwrecks can now be visited by those with the proper training and equipment. Chartered boats offer opportunities for scuba divers to view these historical venues.

A diver climbs aboard the chartered boat *N'Pursuit* after a successful dive in Lake Michigan. *Capt. Mike Tapper, N'Pursuit Adventure Charters. (above)*

The propeller from the wreck *J. D. Marshall* lies next to the pavilion at Indiana Dunes State Park. Several artifacts from that ship are in the state park's Nature Center. *(right)*

The remains of the Alpha Wreck (aka Unknown #4), a ship sunk long ago, appeared on the beach in 1984 when the lake level was extremely low. The hand-hewn timbers suggest that the ship was built between 1860 and 1880. It may have hauled timber from the shore to Chicago. *Bill Warrick*

Wooden structures from the *J. D. Marshall,* an 1891 open-hulled wooden steamer. In 1911, it was retro-fitted as a sand sucker, taking equipment from the *Muskegon.* The next day, June 10, 1911, it sank during a storm. *Indiana Department of Natural Resources*

Iron structures from the *Muskegon*, an 1872 steamer originally named the *Peerless*. The *Muskegon* was destroyed by fire in 1911 while docked at Michigan City and then scuttled in deeper water. Though underwater, the ship now is on the National Register of Historic Places. A few artifacts from the ship are on display at the Old Lighthouse Museum at Michigan City. *Indiana Department of Natural Resources*

## Paddling on Duneland Waters

Paddling northwest Indiana's waterways is a healthy and popular activity. The Northwest Indiana Paddling Association (NWIPA) is actively dedicated to promoting regional paddling and providing environmental stewardship of the region's waterways. It was founded on January 18, 2009, and quickly grew to a membership of more than 350.

The Lake Michigan Water Trail, a route extending from Chicago to New Buffalo, was dedicated as a national recreation trail at a ceremony at the Portage Lakefront and Riverwalk on Saturday, June 4, 2011.

Dan Plath, NWIPA president, called this the first step of a hoped-for shoreline trail all around Lake Michigan. Costa Dillon, superintendent of the Indiana Dunes National Lakeshore, praised the group and its work to make regional waters more accessible to paddlers.

Paddle the Dunes, a 2011 South Shore poster painted by Barbara Spies Labus and sponsored by NIPSCO and NWIPA. *(right) Courtesy of the South Shore Poster Arts Management.*

NWIPA members paddle past the dunes on the new Lake Michigan Water Trail. *(below) Jim Sprandel*

*Adding new life to local rivers and creeks*

On Trail Creek. *(above) Dan Plath*

Jeff Obirek, from the National Park Service Rivers, Trails & Conservation Assistance, and NWIPA member Greg Colton canoe down the east branch of the Little Calumet River. *(left) NWIPA*

## Camping at the State Park

Camping has changed a lot at Indiana Dunes State Park since the campground first opened in the 1930s. The grounds have been recently renovated and have modern restroom and shower facilities. There are 140 campsites, all with 50-amp electrical service, and RVs are permitted. A new shelter for programs has recently been added to the area. The grounds are near the camp store, and nearby trails lead to the beach and to the rest of the park.

There is a separate, private youth camping area designed for Scouts and school, church, and community groups.

The campground at Indiana Dunes State Park.

Camping circa 1930. *(left) Arthur Anderson, Calumet Regional Archives*

A camping area at the National Lakeshore's Dunewood Campground. *(facing)*

A family prepares dinner at the Dunewood Campground. *(facing) NPS, Jeff Manuszak*

## Camping at the National Park

The Dunewood Campground, part of the National Lake-shore, is located in a beautiful wooded area just south of the Dunes Highway (Route 12) in Beverly Shores. It has seventy-eight rather secluded campsites, fifty-three of which are conventional drive-in sites and twenty-five of which are walk-in sites, and a modern restroom and shower building. The grounds are right next to the Dunewood Trace Trail. The South Shore railroad station at Beverly Shores is located about ¼ mile from the campground entrance.

The grounds are open from April 1 to October 31, and RVs are permitted. Registration is on a first-come, first-served basis.

Photographs by Tom Dogan

## Sport Fishing

Fishing has been a popular activity along the shores of Lake Michigan and its tributaries since pre-historic times. In an attempt to sustain commercial and sport fishing, the Indiana Department of Natural Resources Division of Fish and Wildlife began stocking the lake with salmon and trout in the late 1960s. Because of this practice, fishing has taken on new life in Duneland. Anglers line up on good days to fish from various piers along the shore; those who prefer deep-water fishing go out in their boats or contract with the several charter fishing companies located in Portage and Michigan City. Fishing tournaments such the annual Hoosier Coho Club Classic have become popular and give large cash prizes to winners. Nothing is so aggravating as the big ones that got away—except that such happenings are the stimuli for wonderful stories for years to come. But, of course, nothing is as exciting as reeling in a big one and having one's own fish story to tell.

# More Duneland Destinations

In addition to its natural wonders, the Duneland area has plenty of additional places to visit. From its west to its east end, there are places of sculpted and manicured beauty, an English-styled mansion, and futuristic houses as well as llamas, and tigers, and bears.

The Washington Park Zoo entrance plaza.

Director Johnny Martinez in the Australian Aviary.

The grizzly bear exchanges glances with the guests. *(top)*
A peacock shows off his finery. *(middle)*
The WPA Rotary Castle, home of the
amphibians and reptiles. *(bottom)*

## Washington Park Zoo

The Zoo has been a part of Washington Park since 1925—but it has never looked better than it does now. During the Depression, the Works Progress Administration (WPA) built Monkey Island, the Castle, the Observation Tower, and many of the Zoo's winding walkways and stairways. The zoo kept WPA workers so busy that today it has the largest collection of WPA-built leisure structures in Indiana. In 1994, its old observation tower was found to be unsafe and was closed until it was restored and reopened in 2006. (see page 189)

The first decade of the new millennium saw a renewed dedication to making the Zoo a pleasant place for both visitors and the animals. A greater emphasis has been made on interesting and colorful plantings. A new front entrance building containing admissions, a gift shop, and staff offices now welcomes visitors to the Zoo.

New facilities include the bear plaza and the impressive North American carnivore exhibit with its grizzly bears, mountain lions, and river otters in natural-looking environments behind glass-fronted panels. Another new facility is the walk-through Australian Aviary, where visitors can actually enter the "cage" and feed the parakeets. All new exhibits are designed to be as near to nature as possible so as to provide animals with enclosures that allow normal activities.

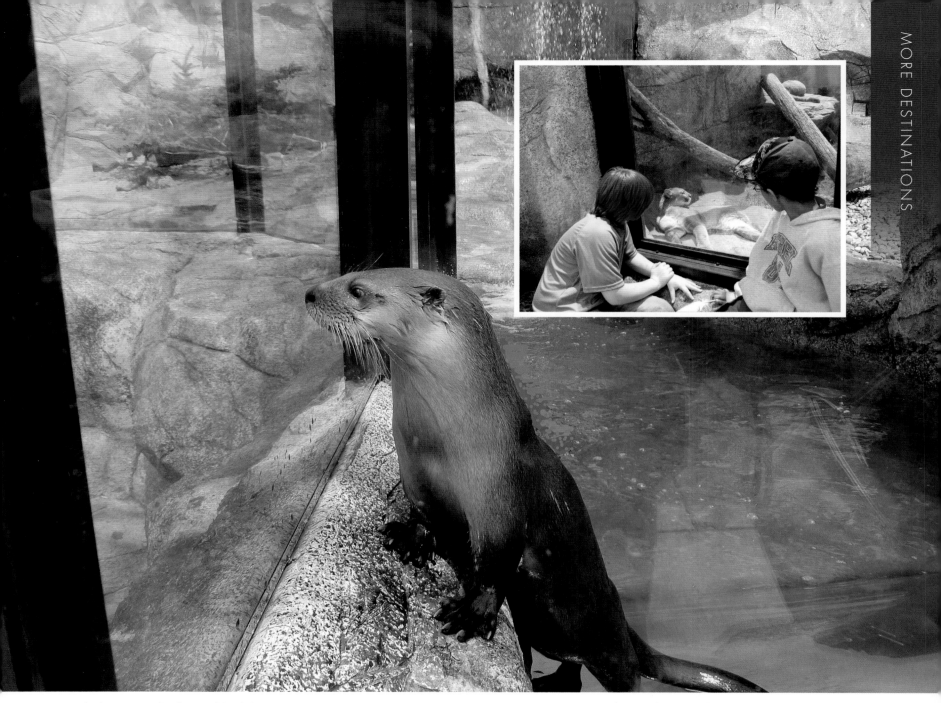

A river otter checks out his visitors.

Up close and personal with a cougar. *(inset)*

The dining room. *(above)*
Michigan City's Barker Mansion. *(right)*
*Both photos by Bj Parmley*

The annual Pink Tea is held in June at the back of the Barker Mansion. Servers were members of the Michigan City High School Senior Honor Society.

## The Barker Mansion

The Barker name is nearly synonymous with Michigan City. According to the Michigan City website, John Barker Sr. arrived in Michigan City in 1836, just as the city was getting started. He worked first as a general merchant, then a grain broker, and finally the owner of a commission house that transferred merchandise from ships at the Michigan City harbor.

Five years after the first railroad came to town, John Sr. bought a railroad car manufacturing business that became known as the Haskell & Barker Car Company. In 1869, John Jr. became general manager. Nineteen years later, he was president. Under the younger Barker's management, the company expanded until it had an annual output of 15,000 cars a year. Barker became wealthy but sadly lost his wife and three infant children. In 1893, Barker married Katherine Fitz-Gerald. Their daughter Catherine was born in 1896. At that time, they decided to enlarge their home at 631 Washington Street.

Chicago architect Frederick Perkins planned the reconstruction, and the new home was completed in 1905. Designed as an

Michigan City's home extraordinaire

The library. *Bj Parmley*

English manor house, it included walnut and mahogany wood-work and fireplaces of hand-carved marble.

Daughter Catherine Barker Hickox, who inherited the house after her parents' death, is remembered as a gracious philanthropist. She established an annuity fund for former Haskell and Barker employees and also the Barker Welfare Foundation.

Although she lived in New York, she restored the mansion and had its original furnishings returned before she donated it to the city in 1968. The house and garden are open for tours and are available for weddings and other special events.

## Century of Progress Homes: A Promising Private/Public Partnership

The Century of Progress Homes on Lakefront Drive in Beverly Shores, built for the 1933 World's Fair in Chicago and transported across the lake when the fair closed, are now owned by the National Park Service. However, by the time they were purchased, the five houses were in rather poor shape—not surprising in that they were only expected to stand for a year or two at the fair. Concerned about their appearance and future, the Historic Landmarks Foundation of Indiana back in the 1980s had placed them on its "most endangered historic sites" list.

In 1986, they were placed on the National Register of Historic Places. In the 1990s, they were leased by the National Park to the Foundation, which agreed to find tenants who would properly restore and then live in the houses. Every autumn, the National Lakeshore hosts an open house during which the houses (completely restored or not) are open to the public.

The Rostone House, also north of the Drive, was originally clad with "Rostone," a synthetic product made to look like natural cut stone. Fortunately, much of the interior also utilized the Rostone material. Although the exterior had disintegrated, the interior had retained its original appearance, making it possible to restore the outside to its original appearance. The house has six rooms.

The Armco-Ferro Enamel House is finished with five-foot wide steel panels covered with porcelain enamel said to be "no thicker than a dime." The construction method was said to be fire resistant, easy to insulate, and inexpensive to maintain. The house was built without rafters, studs, or joists. Large windows allow sunlight to flood the rooms. The four-bedroom house has a roof-top solarium in back.

The House of Tomorrow has probably received the most attention over the years as it somewhat resembles a layer cake. The building is a twelve-sided glass house with neither right angles nor any permanent interior walls except for the bathroom. None of the windows can open because (back in 1933) the house was designed to be air-conditioned. The ground floor originally had space for both a garage and airplane hangar—not terribly useful up on the sand ridge. The second floor has the living quarters while the top floor is a solarium surrounded by an open deck.

The Rostone House.

The Armco-Ferro Enamel House.

The House of Tomorrow.

The Florida Tropical House is hard to miss with its flaming pink exterior north of Lakefront Drive. It is made of reinforced concrete, clay tile, and stucco. The windows are protected by a concrete overlay that shades them in the summer and allows the lower sunlight of winter to shine in. Porthole windows and aluminum rails around a roof-top sundeck were intended to remind one of cruise ships.

The rustic Cypress Log Cabin was sponsored at the fair by the Southern Cypress Growers Association to display the many uses of "pecky" cypress as a building material. Pecky cypress is particularly popular for interior paneling as it has an attractive three-dimensional look unlike any other wood. The home has an 18-by-27-foot great room with cypress paneling and a limestone fireplace.

*Promoting world friendship through plantings*

The Symphony Garden contains a reflecting pool and two fountains. The far end has a canopy that provides protection from rain and sun. This garden, probably the most visited on the grounds, is the scene of the Lyric Opera Series and more than twenty weddings a year.

## International Friendship Gardens

The International Friendship Gardens is the result of a dream of Dr. and Mrs. Frank Warren, developers of the town of Pottawattamie Park. Impressed with the "Peace and Friendship To All Nations" theme of the *Old Mill Garden* at the 1933 Chicago World's Fair, they convinced the garden's creators, Virgil, Joe, and Clarence Stauffer, to re-create their garden east of Michigan City in their new town of Pottawattamie Park. The result was the International Friendship Gardens, which opened to the public two years later.

Throughout its history, the Friendship Gardens has benefited from many volunteers and donors. Great Britain's King George V donated plants and even lent a royal gardener to create an English garden. The Netherlands' Queen Wilhelmina donated 200,000 tulips. All together, there were fourteen formal ethnic gardens, plus the outdoor Theater of Nations built on an island in Lake Lucerne. The theater was the site of many concerts, ballets, and dramas. In the years since, volunteers have donated thousands of dollars and, just as important, thousands of hours of work.

Recent restoration efforts have included a new parking lot, a new service building, and a new greeter's cabin. The number of on-site weddings has increased from nine to twenty-three per year, musical and artistic events are held again, and new heritage gardens have been established.

As noted on its website, the International Friendship Gardens is proud of its achievements and its serene botanical beauty. Visitors from all nations are always welcome.

The United States Steel Chorus and Carrilco Band, directed by Kenneth Resur, performed at the Theater of Nations in 1951. *Calumet Regional Archives*

The Polish Garden with designer and volunteer gardener, Alex Rakowski. *(above)*

The Scottish Garden, honoring Susan Hay Hemminger, first female judge in LaPorte County. *(below) Gene and Romona Hay*

75

*An urban oasis by the lake*

At the time of Father Marquette's visit (1675), this area was near the site of the mouth of the Calumet River. Today, this beautiful lagoon is the source of that river, which now flows toward (instead of from) Illinois.

## Marquette Park

Gary's Marquette Park was created in 1919.

The Bathhouse was built in 1921 and well used for decades, but it closed in the 1960s. It was reopened in 1991, renamed the *Aquatorium,* and restored—as funds have been raised by the newly formed "Society for the Restoration of the Gary Bathing Beach Aquatorium and Octave Chanute's Place in History." It now has a conference room and two museum rooms, one honoring Octave Chanute, whose experiments with gliders took place nearby, and one honoring World War II's Tuskeegee Airmen.

The building was designed by George W. Maher, who, with Frank Lloyd Wright, was a leader of the Prairie School of architecture. One of the first public buildings in the country made of concrete blocks, it is on the National Register of Historic Places.

The Marquette Park Pavilion was built in 1923–24 north of the lagoon that is now the headwaters of the Grand Calumet River. Also designed by George W. Maher, it was renovated in 1966 and again in 2011–12. In its long history, it has been the site of numerous proms, banquets, and wedding receptions.

Father Jacques Marquette's statue has welcomed visitors to "his" park since this sculpture by Henry Hering of New York was dedicated in July 1932. At that same time, the park's name was changed from Lake Front Park to Marquette Park. *(above right) Christopher A. Meyers, City of Gary*

The Aquatorium. *(below)*

The Marquette Park Pavilion. *(right) Christopher A. Meyers, City of Gary*

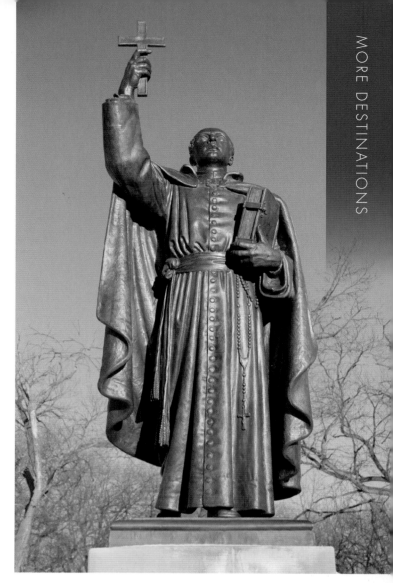

The Dorothy Buell Memorial Visitor Center.

## The Dorothy Buell Memorial Visitor Center

Don't know where to go next? Stop at the Dorothy Buell Visitors Center.

The Center is the result of a partnership of federal, state, and county agencies and serves as the visitor center for the National Lakeshore, the State Park, and Porter County communities. Replacing older visitor centers that were in hard-to-find places, this one is located on Highway 49. It was dedicated in November 2006 and named for Dorothy Richardson Buell, who in 1952 at age sixty-five became the founder, first president, and primary proponent of the Save the Dunes Council.

*The Center includes*
- lobby displays and brochures about Porter County, Indiana Dunes State Park, and Indiana Dunes National Lakeshore,
- the artist in residence exhibit,
- an auditorium where folks can see the video *Child of the Northwest Wind,* and
- the Eastern National bookstore.

# Educational Activities

There is much to learn at the Dunes, and there are many educational opportunities for children, adults, community groups, and families.

Indiana Dunes State Park has the oldest program in the area. It includes self-guided hikes, naturalists who coordinate organized activities for park visitors, and a well designed nature center.

The National Lakeshore has had educational programs since 1968. Its programs focus on both the environmental and cultural resources of the park.

The Dunes Learning Center has had its residential programs since 1998. Private groups such as Save the Dunes, the Izaak Walton League, the Shirley Heinze Land Trust, private and public schools, and Scouting, church, and community groups have all organized their own educational programs.

The pages that follow illustrate just a few of the many opportunities for learning in and about the Dunes.

Paul Quinlan, stewardship director for the Shirley Heinze Land Trust, leads an educational hike. *Ron Trigg*

*Great days outside while learning about nature.*

ParKids learn about the fur trade and pioneers Joseph and Marie Bailly while visiting the Bailly Homestead. *(below)*

ParKids at the Bailly Homestead. *(above)*
*Photos on this page by NPS, Edwin Alcox*

## ParKids at the National Lakeshore

Children spend their days outside exploring the forests, streams, meadows, and trails around the Indiana Dunes National Lakeshore. Some programs include restoration projects. ParKids is a day-camp program at the National Lakeshore where kids from preschool through grade six have fun while learning about plants, animals, ecosystems, art, and history. *NPS (right)*

ParKids learn how to care for their environment and may leave the park in better condition than they found it. *(above) NPS. Photos top and left by NPS, Edwin Alcox*

## Dunes Learning Center: Frog in the Bog

Frog in the Bog is a three-day, two-night experience for grades four through six. During their time at the Center, students are immersed in an exciting outdoor interdisciplinary program that includes science, history, language arts, mathematics, and the fine arts.

Students work in teams and challenge each other. They see, hear, and study wild and beautiful parts of the National Lakeshore that very few people ever visit.

Then students return to their classrooms with memories and data, sketches, and impressions that provide a solid foundation for continued learning. But they also return with an appreciation for their natural environment and a sense of empowerment and responsibility to make a positive difference in their everyday environment.

### DAY 1 · A walk through time

In the afternoon of the first day of camp, students take a walk through Duneland history. Their first stop, pictured above, is at the Bailly Homestead, the actual location of the last Indian trading post in Northwest Indiana. Here they meet a French fur trader (played by a DLC naturalist intern). After this visit, the students meet pioneer farmers, industrialists, environmentalists, and finally a National Park ranger playing him- or herself. *(above) Dunes Learning Center*

### DAY 2 · Hike to the lake on the Cowles Bog Trail

An all-day 4½ mile hike where the students investigate and compare several different ecosystems. *(right) Dunes Learning Center*

DAY 3 · **Park dilemma presentations**

Ranger Ted Winterfeld coordinates group
presentations about dilemmas faced by
park management. *Dunes Learning Center*

## River Quality Activities

Weather permitting, several different educational groups of various ages participate in Hoosier River Watch and other water quality programs. Experiences are different depending on the age and readiness of the participants. These groups were working at the Little Calumet River. *Photos courtesy of Dunes Learning Center.*

*A wet and wild educational experience*

For families, teachers, groups, and individuals

## Adult Education

There are scores of opportunities each year for adults to learn about Duneland. Both the National Lakeshore and the State Park have programs for adults. The Lakeshore working with the Great Lakes Research and Education Center and the Dunes Learning Center offer professional development workshops for teachers and youth group leaders. In addition, private organizations such as Save the Dunes, Friends of Indiana Dunes, Shirley Heinz Land Trust, most Izaak Walton League chapters, and local historical societies offer programs to the public.

Rangers Laura Thompson and Gail Cross take a group of teachers on an interpretive hike. *(top) NPS, Kim Swift*

Every year, IU Northwest biology professor Spencer Cortwright examines the effects of weather on food web health. And each year he takes students or groups from either the National Lakeshore or volunteer organizations with him. This group is made up of volunteers and donors to the Shirley Heinze Land Trust.

This year, there was enough rain to support the growth and reproduction of the many amphibians and insects at the low end of the food chain. Too little rain results in the drying up of shallow wetlands and is detrimental to the reproductive cycle.

IU Northwest Biology professor Spencer Cortwright discusses the effects of weather on food web health with a group of volunteers and donors to the Shirley Heinze Land Trust. *(above) Ron Trigg*

Ranger Wendy Smith points out specific plants on a small group hike. *(left) NPS, Kim Swift*

Tadpoles show that there was sufficient rainfall this last spring. *(below) Ron Trigg*

# Duneland's Industrial Belt

## Port of Indiana—Burns Harbor

Today, the Port of Indiana—Burns Harbor is one of the most modern of all the Great Lakes ports and is home to about thirty companies. The port handles more ocean-going cargo than any other US port on the Great Lakes. Flanked by United States Steel to the west and ArcelorMittal Steel to the east, it handles 15 percent of all US steel trade with Europe. The port has ten steel processing mills on site. In addition to shipping its steel-related cargo, the port supports local farmers by shipping out grains and soybeans while shipping in both liquid and dry fertilizers. The port also handles paper, lumber, salt, limestone, and vehicles. Port officials are quick to remind the public that water-borne transportation is environmentally sound and keeps costs down.

A ship loaded with windmill blades arrives at the port. *(above) Ports of Indiana*

## United States Steel

United States Steel Corporation's Midwest Plant was built beginning in 1959 by the Midwest Steel Company, a subsidiary of National Steel. In 2003, when National Steel declared bankruptcy, the company's assets were purchased by United States Steel.

The Midwest Plant is a finishing facility. It processes steel made primarily at US Steel's Gary Works, about ten miles to the west. The plant has 80" 5-strand cold reduction, temper, and pickle lines in addition to a tin line, a tin-free steel line, a chrome line, and 49" and 72" hot-dip galvanizing lines. The plant produces tin mill products and hot-dip galvanized, cold-rolled, and electrical lamination steels that are used by customers in the construction, container, automotive, and electrical markets. United States Steel employs about nine hundred people at its Midwest plant.

## ArcelorMittal Steel

A fully integrated steel making facility, ArcelorMittal's Burns Harbor plant is one of the company's largest facilities in the United States. The plant operates two blast furnaces and three basic oxygen furnaces that can produce 4.7 million tons of steel each year. It has an 80" hot strip mill and finishing and plate operations. Much of the steel made at this plant is eventually used to make cars and trucks. Other end uses are railroad cars, construction equipment, appliances, and office furniture. The plant has 3,900 employees.

United States Steel Corporation's Midwest Plant.
*United States Steel Corporation*

ArcelorMittal's Burns Harbor plant. The Port of Indiana can be seen to the far left. NIPSCO's Bailly station is at the top center. The highway is Route 12. The National Lakeshore is to the right.
*(below) ArcelorMittal Steel Corporation*

A hot slab of steel ready for processing. *(above)*

Steel coil storage with updated energy-efficient lighting. *(left) Both photos courtesy of Arcelor-Mittal Steel Corporation*

*Bailly generating station*

NIPSCO's Bailly Generating Station, (*above*) and Michigan City Generating Station (*facing top*). NIPSCO

*Michigan City generating station*

Area science teachers touring the inside of the cooling tower in 1973 before it was put into service. *(above)*

Steam from NIPSCO's Bailly Generating Station, blown by a gentle south wind, makes a striking silhouette against the vibrant colors of a Duneland sunset. *(below) Gordon Wilder*

## NIPSCO

The Northern Indiana Public Service Company (NIPSCO), with its headquarters in nearby Merrillville, provides electricity to more than 450,000 customers across the northern third of Indiana. Its Bailly Generating Station is located on a 100-acre site west of Dune Acres. NIPSCO began construction there in 1959, the same year that Midwest Steel began work on its plant east of Burns Ditch. The Station began producing electricity on December 29, 1962. A newer peaking unit went into service in 1968. The units are equipped with various environmental control technologies, including flue gas desulfurization to reduce sulfur dioxide and selective catalytic reduction and overfire air systems to reduce nitrogen oxide emissions.

The nearby Michigan City Generating Station is located on a 134-acre site west of Trail Creek in Michigan City. Michigan City has one coal-fired base-load unit, which went into service in 1974. Hot water from this unit is cooled in its 361-foot natural draft hyperbolic cooling tower. The station also houses two older gas-fired units, which were indefinitely shut down in 2005 due to the age and condition of the boilers.

Most lakeshore activities at the state park end at dusk, but the mills and NIPSCO keep going at full speed 24/7.

# Fine Arts in the Dunes

The Hyndman Gallery at the Lubeznik Center for the Arts. *Rich Manalis*

Five "nymphs" in the 1915 Prairie Club production *The Awakening.* Note the drummer in the background on the left.
*Arthur Anderson, Calumet Regional Archives*

The visual and performing arts have a long history in Duneland. Earl Reed's sketches, Arthur Anderson's photographs, and Frank Dudley's paintings were widely seen and helped spread the word about the dunes and their beauty. "Artie" Anderson's photographs appear throughout this volume. Indeed, this entire book can be thought of as a tribute to the hundreds of photographers and artists who have captured the beauty of Duneland over the years. They've made it possible to enjoy the Dunes, even when one is away from them.

Michigan City's Silver Cornet Band got its start in 1869. Dance bands entertained both young and old at Carr's Beach and at Washington Park more than a hundred years ago. The Prairie Club had a history of pageants in the dunes before its huge 1917 pageant, *The Dunes Under Four Flags.*

The Beverly Shores theater brought in actors from Chicago's Goodman Theater for productions throughout the summers from 1935–41. When it closed, several of its organizers then started the Dunes Summer Theater and the Footlight Players. Both Miller and Furnessville have long attracted artists.

Michigan City's Lubeznik Center for the Arts is now a magnet for artists and art lovers throughout the region. Miller held its first "Massive Art Attack: Pop Up Art on Lake Street" in 2011. Its Lake Street Gallery provided for this book many historical photographs.

As can be seen on the following pages, the fine arts have changed, but they are still alive and healthy in Duneland.

*A Storm in the Dunes.*

### Earl H. Reed

Earl H. Reed (1863–1931) loved wandering in the Dunes, experiencing the region's sights and smells, talking to its residents, and recording his thoughts in prose, poetry, and through his sketches. With a minimum of pen strokes, he could create an evocative scene of dunes and clouds responding to the swirling lakeshore winds.

Reed was the author of several illustrated books including *The Voices of the Dunes, and other Etchings* (1912), *The Dune Country* (1916), and *Sketches in Duneland* (1918).

As an author, a poet, and an artist, he played a great part in describing to the nation the beauties of the Dunes.

*Among the Sand Hills.*

*When the night shadows come into the dune country,*
*the spell of mystery and poetry comes with them.*
*The sorcery of the dark places*
*leads us into a land of dreams and unreality.*

—EARL H. REED,
*The Dune Country*, 1916

*Heralds of the Storm. All photos on both pages courtesy of Save the Dunes.*

*The gull has many charms for the ornithologist and the poet. He is valuable to the artist, as an accent in the sky, when he is on the wing, giving a thrill of life to the most desolate landscape.*

*He is interesting to the eye when proudly walking along the beach, or sitting silently, with hundreds of others, in solemn conclave on the shore.*

*The perched birds seem magnified and ghostly when one comes suddenly upon them in the fog and they disappear with shrill cries into the mists.*

*They are the heralds of the storms and a typical expression of life in the sky.*

—EARL H. REED,
*The Dune Country,* 1916

## The Gingrich Colorized Glass Slides

William F. Gingrich (1874–1959), a Chicago schoolteacher and principal, spent many hours photographing the dunes. He recorded Duneland scenery on glass slides, which he then painted to give them color. *All images courtesy of Ogden Dunes Historical Society*

*Phlox Divaricata (above) and Interdunal Pond. (below)*

*Moving Dune. (above)*

*Trees.*

*Waiting for the train, Tremont, Indiana.*

*Loading the bicycles, Tremont, Indiana.*

## The Norman Bergendahl Colorized Prints

Norman Bergendahl (1906–1989) was a naturalist who conducted much of his research in the dunes. He photographed the area extensively, but his most intriguing photos are the ones that he colorized. Two of his most interesting photos were taken on an organized bike ride to the dunes. *(Calumet Regional Archives)*

## Frank V. Dudley

Frank V. Dudley (1868–1957) is history's most prominent painter of the Dunes. Beginning in 1911 and continuing for more than 40 years, Dudley wandered through the dunes setting up his easel on the beach, on the dune tops, in the woods. He moved his studio to where Indiana Dunes State Park is today. He advocated for the preservation of the dunes and at the age of 85 served on an advisory board for the Save the Dunes Council. After his death, Council members carried many of his paintings to the

*The Land of Sky and Song*, 1918, oil on canvas, 45×60 inches. *Frank V. Dudley* © *Brauer Museum of Art, Valparaiso University*

The Magic Hour, 1950, oil on canvas,
20×22 inches. *Frank V. Dudley*
© *Brauer Museum of Art,*
*Valparaiso University*

## Artist and activist for the dunes

congressional meeting rooms where hearings were held on the pro-
posal to establish a national park. Curator Richard H. W. Brauer
said that "when most people saw the dunes as sandy wastes unfit
for art or most anything else, Dudley, on the contrary, was among
those who saw the dunes as beautiful and inspiring, and became
foremost in painting their beauty."

99

*Sandland's Even Song,* 1920, oil on board, 38×50 inches.
*Frank V. Dudley © Brauer Museum of Art, Valparaiso University*

*Tremont,* 1923, oil on canvas, 30×40 inches.
*Frank V. Dudley © Brauer Museum of Art, Valparaiso University*

## The Artist in Residence Program

*Marikay Peter Witlock—2002 artist*

The federal government has a long history of commissioning photographers and artists to record cultural and natural landscapes. The Indiana Dunes National Lakeshore continues that tradition through its Artist in Residence Program.

Each summer, the National Lakeshore provides a residence in the dunes area to selected artists so that they may experience one of the most environmentally diverse parks in the country and use their time to be creative. In exchange, the artists provide a framed piece of art at the end of the residency and give a public presentation of their work.

The works on these four pages were created as part of Marikay Peter Witlock's residency. During her residency, Ms. Witlock visited all parts of the National Lakeshore, working to capture the diversity of the park. The following year, Witlock presented *Paintings from the Dunes: Fifty Paintings from the Indiana Dunes National Lakeshore* at the Union Street Gallery in Chicago Heights, Illinois.

*Beach Series no. 5,* 2003, soft pastel, 9×6 inches. *Marikay Peter Witlock*

*Water's Edge no. 3,* 2000, soft pastel, 21×7 inches. *Marikay Peter Witlock (facing left)*

*Moonrise at Long Lake,* 2002, soft pastel, 12×14 inches. *Marikay Peter Witlock (facing right)*

*Dune Central Beach, no. 3, 2002,*
soft pastel, 14.5×9.5 inches.
*Marikay Peter Witlock*

*Dune Central Beach, no. 6,* 2003,
soft pastel, 17×11.5 inches.
*Marikay Peter Witlock*

## Children's theater programs

*Tom Sawyer. (above)*

*Yankee Doodle. (above right)*

*All photos on both pages courtesy of Dunes Summer Theater*

### Duneland Dramatics

There is something about Duneland that inspires dreams of fantasy and drama through the performing arts. Live theater has been an important part of Duneland life since an outdoor Prairie Club performance in 1913. Few other parts of the country, outside of our great cities, can boast of three locations hosting long-established theater programs.

As noted years back in Michigan City's *News Dispatch*, "the cast may be composed of children, but there's nothing childish about children's theatre productions." In 1948, local playwright Nora Tully MacAlvay organized the first children's theater in the area. Three years later, her program was made part of the then-new Dunes Arts Foundation. In the summer, this still-strong program uses the Dunes Summer Theater building, but for the rest of the year, classes are held in Michigan City.

## Dunes Summer Theater

Dunes Summer Theater traces its history back to 1939, when the Michiana Shores Theater Colony ran a dramatic school and held performances on Saturday evenings. The 360-seat theater building used today and the adjacent cabins were built in 1940.

When Nora Tully MacAlvay discovered that the Michiana theater was for sale in 1951, she helped organize the Dunes Arts Foundation. Since then, the Foundation has organized and run a series of dramatic plays and musicals each summer. College students (primarily theater majors) are recruited each year to live at the theater center, build sets, and help wherever needed. The Foundation celebrated its sixtieth anniversary in 2011.

The Dunes Summer Theater building. *(top)*

*Joseph and the Amazing Technicolor Dreamcoat. (middle)*

*Driving Miss Daisy. (left)*

## Footlight Players:
## Community theater in a "Subway"

The Footlight Players group got its start in 1950 with a production of *Laura* at the Coolspring Township's Institute Hall on South Johnson Road. (The first musical was *The Mikado* in 1958.) Since *Laura*, this local theater group has continued to entertain the Michigan City area for more than sixty years. Now in its own theater building (a former Subway restaurant—completely re-modeled), the Footlight Players group produces five to six plays and musicals a year in a season extending from September to June.

*Dixie Swim Club (above)* and *Nunsense. (below)*
*Photos courtesy of Footlight Players*

# Canterbury summer theater / Mainstreet theater

## Festival Players Guild

In 1969, Michigan City businessman Lyman Taylor purchased the St. John's Lutheran Church building on Franklin Street, christened it the Canterbury Theater, and founded the Festival Players Guild. For the first twenty-eight years of its existence, the guild performed at the Canterbury. After the Canterbury was sold, productions were moved to 807 Franklin Street, an old storefront that was renovated to create an intimate theater complex while maintaining much of the flavor of the original building, including its tin ceiling.

The Mainstreet Theater hosts an intensive "resident" company summer stock series called the Canterbury Summer Theater and a winter arts series consisting of both plays and concerts. The Canterbury actors come from all over the country. Many are college students preparing for professional acting careers.

*Spitfire Grill (top)* and *The Secret Garden. (left)*
*Festival Players Guild*

A city tradition since 1869

The band at The Guy Foreman
Bicentennial Amphitheatre. *(top)*

Director Rick D'Arcangelis. *(below left)*

*All photos on both pages courtesy
of MC Municipal Band*

## Michigan City Municipal Band

The sounds of music flow across Washington Park on Thursday
nights in Michigan City. Since 1869, Michigan City has had a
municipal band. Although it's had different names over the years,
the purpose has been the same: to develop and use the talents
of the musicians as they entertain and enlighten local citizens.

Steve Hornyak (timpani) is the current band president, and
Rick D'Arcangelis, a music teacher at Barker Middle School, is
the director. The band usually plays in the Guy Foreman Bicentennial Amphitheater, named for a long-time former band
director, but for the Independence Day concert it plays at
the park's old band shell.

Trumpet.

Sax.

Timpani.

Cymbals.

Clarinet.

# Stormy Weather

Gathering storm clouds at Portage Lakefront and Riverwalk. *Fredric Young*

*When the storm gods lash the lake with whistling winds,*
*and send their sullen dark array through the skies,*
*and the music of the tempest blends*
*with song of surges on the shore,*
*the color tones seem to become vocal*
*and mingle their cadences with the voices of the gale.*

—EARL H. REED, *The Dune Country*, 1916

And, of course, there were two brave photographers
this stormy day. *NPS, Edwin Alcox*

*When only the brave or foolhardy take photographs*

Central Beach Storm.
*NPS, Edwin Alcox*

Storm clouds arrive at
the marina at Michigan
City. *Tom Dogan*

# Autumn Leaves and Shortening Days

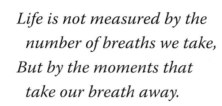

*Life is not measured by the
number of breaths we take,
But by the moments that
take our breath away.*

—ANON

## An Annual Collage of Color

The warm days, cool nights, and spectacular colors make Duneland a delight in autumn. Crowds thin at the beach, and school groups begin their annual treks to one of the most beautiful places in the Midwest.

*When I was in my teens I used to love hiking.
Always a bunch of girlfriends and I would set
out for a whole day of hiking in the woods.*

—LILLIAN WESTERGREN WEIGER,
who lived not far from Green Heron Pond

The Chellberg Farmhouse. *(top) Jim Rettker*
Along the Calumet Trail. *(middle) Ron Trigg*
Green Heron Pond, Miller. *(bottom) Ron Trigg*

*A time to give thanks and to prepare for spring*

The White Bridge, the focal point of the Celebration Gardens of the International Friendship Gardens, has striking beauty in all seasons, but perhaps particularly in the fall. *International Friendship Gardens*

## Thoughts of Tulips and Turkeys

Fall is a busy time at the International Friendship Gardens. It the time for teaching kids how to plant spring-flowering bulbs and a time to celebrate Thanksgiving by inviting the community to the annual Turkey Walk.

On Thanksgiving Day, the community is invited to stroll through the gardens between ten AM and four PM, to enjoy the fresh air and either work up an appetite or walk off their second helping of dinner. Donations of foods are collected for those in need. The day also includes a children's hunt for paper turkeys hidden in the woods.

*All photos by International Friendship Gardens*

Sassafras leaves in autumn are a favorite, especially for children. Their bright orange leaves and stark black bark reflect the colors of the Halloween season.

Sassafras leaves come in three shapes—all on the same tree.

- Oval leaves are the shape of footballs—a favorite autumn sport.
- Leaves with two lobes, one large and one small, remind us of mittens that come out of the closet this time of year.
- Leaves with three lobes bring to mind friendly ghosts. Whoooooooooo.

Sassafras leaves. *Ron Trigg*

The Svenska Skola on
Oak Hill Road. *Jim Rettker*

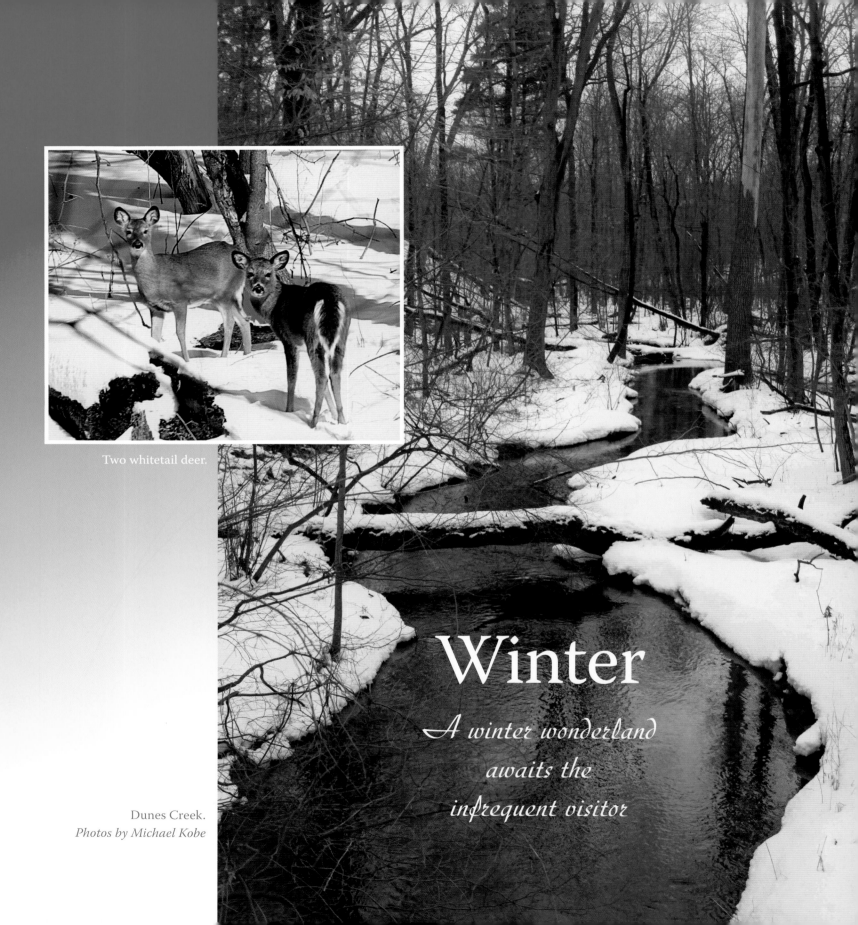

Two whitetail deer.

Dunes Creek.
*Photos by Michael Kobe*

# Winter

*A winter wonderland*

*awaits the*

*infrequent visitor*

Snowy spruces. *(above) Michael Kobe*

Winter storms at Ogden Dunes. *(right) Tom Dogan*

A snowstorm at Ogden Dunes. *(above) Tony Gaul*

The Burstrom Chapel (or Svenska Skola) in winter. *(left) Michael Kobe*

Leaving home can be an adventure (Beverly Shores).
*(above) Tom Dogan*

Michigan City Lighthouse. *(left) Tom Dogan*

Mallards. *Michael Kobe*

Almost a lunar landscape at the
Dunes State Park beach. *Carol Wood*

*Winter Solace. Pete Doherty, Doherty Images*

## Annual Lucia Pageant

On the old Julian calendar, Saint Lucia Day, December 13th, was the winter solstice—the shortest and darkest day of the year. Winters are long and dark in Scandinavia, and so it is not surprising that a winter celebration of light would become popular there—and among Scandinavians who came to America. This certainly included the Chellbergs and the other Swedish immigrant pioneers who came to Duneland in the middle of the nineteenth century.

On St. Lucia Day, a daughter dresses in white and, wearing a crown of lighted candles (battery-powered today), wakes her parents with coffee and Santa Lucia buns. The tradition was re-initiated at the Chellberg farm in 1980 and has become an annual tradition.

The Chellberg Farmhouse in winter.
*(above) Zella Olson*

Christina Birky, the 2010 Santa Lucia.
*(left) Michael T. Gard*

*Celebrating the life of a saint who cared for others*

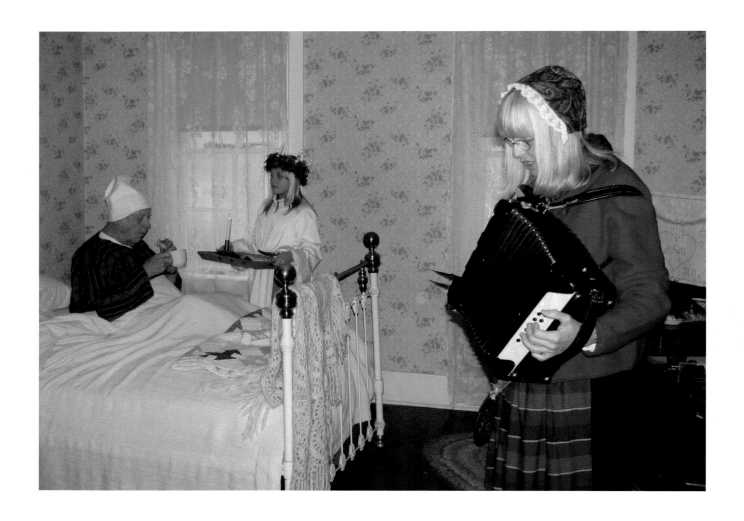

Christina Birky demonstrates how "Santa Lucia" would serve her parents coffee and Santa Lucia buns while still in bed. Here Christina's "grandfather" enjoys the treats while Marti Pizzini plays *Santa Lucia* on the accordion. Grandfather is portrayed by Henry Studebaker, himself the son of Naomi Chellberg Studebaker, who many years ago played the part of Lucia when she was a child in this very house. *Diana Birky*

*Getting there is half the experience*

## Cross-Country Skiing

The Dunes Learning Center runs a popular school program throughout the winter months called "Winter Survival in the Dunes." When there's enough snow on the ground, kids use cross-country skis on their hikes.

Almost-proficient students ski back to the Center through a winter wonderland.
*(above) Dunes Learning Center*

Students quickly learn that skiing is fun.
*(right) Michael Kobe*

When winter lays its mantle of snow
  upon the country of the dunes,
the whitened crests loom in softened lines.
Along the frosty summits, the intricacies
  of the naked trees and branches
are woven delicately against the moody skies,
and the hills stand in faint relief on the
  gray horizon.

—EARL H. REED, *The Dune Country*, 1916

*Dunes State Park pavilion area at dusk.*
*(facing) Kim Swift, NPS*

PART TWO
*Stories of Duneland*

Beach-goers, 1933.
*Michael N. Kobe*

# Indian Life in the Dunes Before 1833

The Potawatomi culture, like most American Indian cultures, was complex, with traditions that created a sense of closeness to nature. The Potawatomi were both hunters and farmers. However, before contact with Europeans, they had no steel axes or plows, so they could not clear forests or cut through thick prairie sod. Instead, they often planted their seeds in the soft soils beside streams and rivers.

Although the Potawatomi set up camp along the Lake Michigan shoreline in summer, there were no permanent Indian villages along the beach or in the dunes. The beach offered no protection, and few foods could be grown on the sand dunes. Thus,

Shabbona. *Gary Public Library*

many Potawatomi villages were located alongside the rivers and lakes of the Calumet and Kankakee areas, where fresh food and water were available. The Potawatomi spent the winters near the Kankakee River, away from the snow belt and the harsh weather conditions near Lake Michigan.

Indians traded with Jean Baptiste Point de Sable, who had a trading post on Trail Creek in the 1770s, and also with Joseph Bailly in the 1820s. Shabbona, said to be Marie Bailly's cousin, was a Potawatomi chief best known as the "Peace Chief." He was a frequent visitor at the Bailly Homestead.

## A Boy's Memories of Witnessing Indian Life

I had an opportunity to visit the Indian wigwams on the shore of Lake Michigan in the summer and fall of 1837—to see the women at their work, the children at their play, the fires in the centers of their frail structures and the hunters as they returned from a successful chase. I saw their roasted venison and had an opportunity to partake of it. I saw their large birch-bark canoes and the Indian boys of my own age spearing fish. I often saw parties of Indian men riding on their ponies one after the other in true Indian file; and I saw some of them in the attitude of mourners beside some graves at a little Indian burial ground.

A similar life, with some quarrels and strife, some scenes perhaps of war and bloodshed, we may suppose the Red Men to have passed for the last two hundred years. For them the Calumet Area must have been peculiarly attractive as furnishing so many muskrats and mink for fur, so many fish and waterfowls for food.

*—Attributed to Timothy Ball (1826–1913)*

For the Indians, as for white settlers, geography dictated transportation routes. Because of the east-west orientation of rivers, shorelines, and moraines south of Lake Michigan, north-south travel across them was difficult at best. East-west travel was easier. For this the Indians used the lakeshore as well as the ancient shorelines. The region's most famous trail, the Sauk Trail, had a north branch that split from the main trail at what is now West-ville and ran through Baileytown to Lake Michigan.

The Potawatomi Trail is a name informally given to many local Indian trails. In one sense, all the trails were Potawatomi trails. The best known extended through LaPorte, Baileytown, Portage, Lake Station, and Dyer.

Many Indian trails became wagon and stage-coach routes. Years later, when the new counties needed to build roads through the area, the first routes chosen often followed these trails. Albert Scharf noted that the Indian trail became "first a bridle path, then a public highway, a stage and mail route along which the main streets of many towns were subsequently laid out."

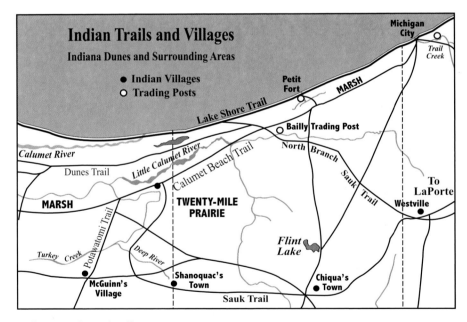

Indian Trails and Villages.
*K. J. Schoon, 2012 (above)*

Potawatomi Trail marker on Indiana
Highway 51 south of Interstate 94. *(left)*

# 1675 French Connections

It is probably impossible to know who were the first Europeans to visit Duneland. In 1667, Father Claude Allouez referred to the "yet unexplored" Lake Michigan. However, it can be assumed that the first were French Canadian coureurs des bois (runners of the woods), fur trappers who worked without a license from the French government. Because their work was illegal, these hardy folks did not make written records. However, it is very likely that the Calumet Area, with its wealth of wildlife, would have been known to them. Two coureurs des bois met Father Jacques Marquette in December 1674 when he encamped at Chicago. After 1681, the government began licensing a limited number of these men. These legal travelers were called "voyageurs."

## Jacques Marquette and Louis Jolliet

Father Jacques Marquette is by far the best known of the French missionaries who explored the south Lake Michigan area, and his exploration in 1673 is the earliest of which there are any written records. That summer, Marquette and Louis Jolliet explored the Mississippi valley from Wisconsin to as far south as Arkansas. On their return trip, they came up the Illinois River, crossed the Chicago portage, and canoed down to the mouth of the Chicago River. Marquette was evidently pleased with his reception by the Illinois Indians, and he promised that he would return.

In the autumn of the following year, Father Marquette returned to Illinois. He and two companions spent the 1674–75 winter camped at the portage of the Chicago and Des Plaines Rivers. Marquette had been very ill during much of this trip, but by March he was well enough to travel down the Illinois River and preach to the Illinois Indians at the village of Kaskaskia (near modern-day Utica). However, by April he was much worse and soon lost almost all of his strength.

As Marquette sensed that he was dying, he wished to quickly return to his mission at the Straits of Mackinac. So he cut short his trip and, accompanied by many of the Illini, paddled up the Illinois River toward Lake Michigan.

Father Jacques Marquette. *NPS*

## Marquette's Trip through Northwest Indiana

Although we know that Marquette's party paddled up the east shore of the lake, his exact route through Indiana is unknown. Marquette kept a diary of careful notes about his travels, but his last entry was made at Kaskaskia. The account of his return trip was written two years later by Father Claude Dablon, who probably got his information from Marquette's companions. Dablon notes that Marquette reached the lake of the Illinois (Lake Michigan) and "was obliged to coast along the southern Shore. . . ." Dablon also noted that Marquette at this time was "so feeble and exhausted that he was unable to assist or even move himself, and had to be handled and carried about like a child."

Ulrich Danckers, in his *Early Chicago* (1999), described the route as "by way of Hickory Creek [and Thorn Creek] to the Calumet River and Lake Michigan." Using this route, Marquette's group would have entered Lake Michigan at the mouth of the Calumet River at what is now Gary's Marquette Park.

Since his group paddled an average of thirteen miles each day, it probably would have stopped for the night at three places along the Indiana portion of the lakeshore. The three most likely places would have been at the mouths of the Calumet River (at Gary's Marquette Park), Fort or Dunes Creek (Dunes State Park), and Trail Creek (now Michigan City). Powell Moore noted, "It is even probable that they camped at the mouth of the Grand Calumet and that Mass was celebrated there, as so many believe."

George Brennan, in his *Wonders of the Dunes* (1928), described Marquette's trip in great detail. Although there is no written documentation to substantiate his stories, they have become part of the lore of the Dunes region:

> As he journeyed, he stopped frequently and took shelter in the different creeks and rivers that pierced the Dunes, camping there overnight and also in bad weather. He preached often to the Indians, and camped on the shores of the Calumet River, Fort Creek, Trail Creek— the Rivière du Chemin—St. Joe and others.
>
> It is stated by Mr. Coughlan, who heard it from the Indians, that when Marquette stopped at Trail Creek, a delegation of Indians who had heard him preach before met him and begged him to come up to

their village a short distance away. He did so and found that they had a village in a most beautiful grove and plateau called Council Grove, which now [1923] belongs to ex-Mayor Martin T. Krueger of Michigan City (a friend of Brennan's) and is part of his Springland Farm.

On the western slope of this historic plateau is a spring (now at the International Friendship Gardens), which Marquette blessed, and which the Indians called Marquette Spring. For many years, this was the Mecca of the Indian tribes who came for miles to get the water of that spring, which they said was "good medicine."

Mr. Daniel Kelly, of Valparaiso, an eminent lawyer has a relic that speaks of the early missionaries. It is the silver lid of a small lavorium or baptismal font, used by priests to baptize new members, and was found in the dried-up bed of the old mouth of the Grand Calumet River at Miller. Mr. Kelly consulted several authorities, even sending the lavorium to Paris. He was told that it was evidently made in the sixteenth century. Another piece of lavorium was found near the same spot some years before by Father Goodman, who sent it to the Paris Historical Society.

Note: While hoping to be able to get a photograph of the lavorium, I contacted relatives of Mr. Kelly, who unfortunately had no knowledge of it or of this story. KS.

Father Marquette, not yet thirty-eight years old, didn't make it to the mission. He died a couple of weeks later and was buried near what is now Ludington, Michigan, along the banks of the river now known as the Pere Marquette.

The fur trade was very profitable for the French, who protected that trade with a series of forts built between Montreal and New Orleans. Those near the Calumet Area were Fort St. Joseph on the St. Joseph River north of present-day South Bend, a second fort on the Chicago River, and a third apparently built in 1693 near the south end of Lake Michigan and abandoned three years later. In addition to forts, there were numerous stockaded log cabins built by trappers such as Le Petit Fort, built about 1750, at what is now Indiana Dunes State Park.

## Voyageurs

As the fur trade grew, it was impossible for local Indians to take enough pelts to Montreal to satisfy the European demand for furs. Thus, beginning in about 1690, the fur companies began to hire

men to travel into the wilderness to trade with the Indians and to then take back the desired pelts. These men were the "voyageurs," and they soon became the circulatory system of the fur trade.

Voyageurs have been romanticized in Canadian and American popular culture as rugged and self-reliant, adventuresome, competitive, prideful, and sometimes boastful. Canadian journalist Peter Newman noted that their eighteen-hour paddling days were "more wretched than many men now or then could survive" adding that "no voyageur ever reported meeting a small bear, a tame moose, or a wolf that wasn't snarling with blood-lust."

In truth, voyageurs were a diverse and very complex labor force. They were known for their singing, a trait that helped them not only pace themselves while paddling but also celebrate their adventures, their loves, and their homes back east. Their jobs were dangerous, and many died from disease, accidents, and

Thomas Wojcinski, a member of Les Habitants du Petit Fort, portraying a French fur trader of the 1670s. All the materials a man like this needed would be packed and transported in his canoe. *Elaine Wojcinski*

attacks by unfriendly Indians. Some quit, but most served out their contracts and returned to their families, settled down, and resumed "normal" lives.

## Le Petit Fort

Le Petit Fort is a northwest Indiana mystery. That it did exist is certain. Who built it and when, and exactly where it was, are still unknown.

Rather than being a military structure, Le Petit Fort was a small French trading post surrounded by a stockade. Inside the stockade would have been a garden and a cabin for sleeping and the storing of furs. The stockade would have kept deer away from the young plants. The cabin probably had no stone fireplace, as remains of such would probably have been found by now.

As the fur trade continued into the 1820s, it is possible that Le Petit Fort continued to be used, perhaps temporarily, as a storage and living area. In any event it was still standing in 1803 when Lieutenant James Swearington noted in a report that his men had camped near the "old fort." The fort also appears on a map of the area drawn by General William Hull, who was stationed near the area in 1812.

The "fort" was located somewhere near the mouth of Fort Creek (today Dunes Creek at Dunes State Park). Hull's map shows it inland a bit. Historian George Brennan claimed in 1923 that he had located the site of the fort, saying that it was "on a high bluff about a half mile southwest of Mount Tom."

## The End of the Era

The Potawatomi way of life was permanently changed after contact with the French. Before beginning to trade with the French, the Indians were generally self-sufficient. The Potawatomi did trade excess corn to tribes from the north, but they did not depend upon trade for needed supplies. However, French traders wanted furs, which the Indians could provide, and the Indians soon wanted the metal utensils, guns, gunpowder, and alcohol that the French were willing to trade.

The French and Indian War (1754–63) ended French control of northern North America. France ceded its lands east of the

Le Petit Fort of the 1750s may have looked similar to, but likely was cruder than, the Officers' Mess at this reconstruction of the 1758 Fort Ligonier in Pennsylvania. *Fort Ligonier*

General William Hull's map of 1812 as shown in George Brennan's book *The Wonders of the Dunes.*

Mississippi to Britain, and thus British soldiers replaced French soldiers in many Midwestern forts.

Scattered reminders of the French period exist today throughout the dunes and surrounding areas. Marquette Park, several Marquette Streets, and Marquette schools commemorate the famous missionary. Joliet, Illinois, sits on the Des Plaines River (French for "of the plains"). Several nearby communities have Joliet Streets. Local railroads have used both Marquette and Joliet in their names. LaPorte ("the door") refers to the passageway in the old forests that led from the east to the Calumet Area.

## 1775 Jean Baptiste Point de Sable

The first known non-Indian resident in the Calumet Area (and later the first settler of what would become Chicago) was the black fur trader Jean Baptiste Point de Sable, a French- and Algonquin-speaking British subject. For a short time between 1775 and 1779, Point de Sable and his Potawatomi wife Catherine ran a trading post on the Rivière du Chemin (Trail Creek) at the present-day site of Michigan City. During the Revolutionary War, Point de Sable (who was not known as "Du Sable" until after his death) was accused of being an American sympathizer and in 1779 was arrested by British forces. He was taken to Michilimackinac, where, cleared of all charges, he served as a member of the British Indian Department. No physical trace of his trading post has been found along Trail Creek.

## 1780 The Battle of the Dunes

The Duneland area was the site of a Revolutionary War skirmish on December 5, 1780. Apparently inspired by George Rogers Clark's victory over the British at Vincennes, a group of sixteen men from the Cahokia area in Illinois, commanded by Jean Baptiste Hammelin (a French Canadian who fought for the United States), raided the British Fort St. Joseph (at present-day Niles, Michigan). Arriving when the British commander and most of the Potawatomi residents were out on a winter hunt, they loaded their packhorses with furs taken from the fort and began the slow

Historical marker at Dunes State Park.

Historical marker at Michigan City.

1. Indiana University Northwest history professor Powell Moore described the event as being at Le Petit Fort on Fort (Dunes) Creek. He was aware that George Brennan (thirty-six years earlier) believed it to have been at Trail Creek, but he thought that the evidence for Fort Creek was stronger.

trek back west along the lakeshore. When the British commander arrived back at the fort, he gathered a group of loyal Potawatomi Indians, and they gave pursuit.

They caught up with the American raiders either at Trail Creek or Le Petit Fort[1] and ordered them to surrender. When the Americans refused, the skirmish began. In the words of the only written description of the battle, "Without a loss of a man on [the British] side, [they] killed four, wounded two, and took seven Prisoners, the other three escaped in the thick Wood." The prisoners were treated as thieves, rather than prisoners of war, since none of them were found to have an army commission. Thomas Brady, formerly a superintendent of Indian Affairs, was one of those taken prisoner. It is believed by many that Mt. Tom, the highest dune in the region, is named for him.

On May 20, 1957, the Daughters of the American Revolution dedicated a historical monument at Dunes State Park commemorating the 1780 Battle of the Dunes. Because of some conflicting evidence, author George Brennan and others have believed that the battle took place in the Michigan City area. The Colonial Dames erected a similar marker at Michigan City's Krueger Park.

## 1822 The Bailly Homestead

Joseph Bailly was a French Canadian born in Quebec in 1774. His wife, Marie, was of French and Ottawa Indian parentage. In 1822 they and their children moved to Potawatomi country in Duneland. They established their home and trading post on the north bank of the Little Calumet River near where the north branch of the Sauk Trail crossed both the river and the Calumet Beach Trail (now the Dunes Highway). In this strategic location, their home could be reached by canoe and by foot. After the home was badly damaged by floodwaters, they moved to higher ground but remained close to the river.

Bailly had a successful business with the Indians. He received furs from them, which he traded for items from Mackinac and Detroit. Marie, who always dressed in Indian clothing, was as familiar with Indian ways as she was with the French. This undoubtedly helped them in their dealings with the Potawatomi.

Within ten years, Bailly had six to eight cabins for his French employees. For those years, the Baillys were the only settlers in the Calumet Area. Their home was the center of culture and civilization in the Calumet Area wilderness. The Baillys welcomed all travelers, missionaries, and Indians.

The Bailly homestead was a welcome sight for the occasional travelers going to or from Detroit to Fort Dearborn (Chicago) and other points west. Ottawa and Potawatomi Indians were the most frequent visitors. According to the Baillys' granddaughter, Frances Howe, Joseph traded with the Indians and sent his furs to Mackinac in barge-like rowboats on Lake Michigan. On occasion, he would travel to Quebec or Baton Rouge, where he would receive pelts from the west.

Bailly's business ventures were successful, and in 1834 he had a large frame house erected. As he could see that the fur-trading era was coming to a close, Bailly began investing in land. He purchased more than two thousand acres, made plans for a harbor on Lake Michigan, and in December of 1833 laid out plans for what he called the "Town of Bailly" about one mile west of the homestead. To this day, the area around that site as well as the homestead is informally called "Bailey Town" (for some reason with a different spelling of his name).

Joseph Bailly died in 1835; Marie survived him by thirty-one years. It is believed that Monee, Illinois, is named for her.

The house and grounds have been altered a great deal since Joseph and Marie's time. The house was remodeled after Marie Bailly's death in 1866 and then again around 1900, when the front and rear porches were added. Behind the main house is a red brick building that was built around 1874 by the Baillys' granddaughter Rose Howe. Originally attached to the southeast corner of the house, the ground floor was a kitchen while the second floor was Rose's studio. The house was moved to its present location in 1904.

There are three log buildings on the grounds today: the chapel, southwest of the main house; a two-story log building built from the remains of the Bailly's dairy house and tool shed; and the fur traders' cabin or storehouse. It was made of logs from the original storehouse in which Joseph Bailly invited Indians to leave their belongings while away hunting.

The Bailly house, built in 1835, restored to its appearance in 1917—the year the last Bailly family member to live there died. To the left are two of the log cabins that have been restored to their fur-trading-era appearance. *Jim Rettker*

The tombstones of Joseph and Marie Bailly (left) and their son-in-law Francis Howe and daughter Rose set into the wall surrounding the Bailly Cemetery. *Jim Rettker*

In 1907, Frances Howe put her memories of the homestead into words and published the booklet *The Story of a French Homestead in the Old Northwest.* The book did not sell well, and, despondent, Frances burned all the unsold books. (Fortunately, the book was republished in 1999.) Frances was the last of the family to live at the homestead. After she died in 1918, the property and furnishings were sold. Since then, there have been several owners of the homestead and cemetery. For a few years after 1965, the "Big House" was even used as a restaurant, the Homestead Inn.

In 1958, a group of historians and environmentalists investigated purchasing the property because of its historical significance. That didn't happen in spite of the fact that the owner appeared willing to sell. Nevertheless, four years later, the property was declared a National Historic Landmark. It was purchased by the National Park Service in 1971 and became one of the first properties of the National Lakeshore.

The site and cemetery have been restored and are now used as interpretive centers of the Indiana Dunes National Lakeshore. The Homestead is visited year-round by school groups, students at the Dunes Learning Center, ParKids (day camp participants), and other visitors.

## The Bailly Cemetery

In 1827, Joseph and Marie Bailly's son Robert caught typhoid fever and died. Robert was buried three-quarters of a mile north of the homestead on a high dune just south of the old Chicago–Detroit Road, now Route 12 (the ancient Calumet Shoreline of Lake Michigan).

The Baillys didn't own this land in 1827, as no land in northwest Indiana had yet been put up for sale by the US government. So in years to come, neighbors, including the many Swedish families that lived nearby, also used this sandy area for their burials as well. This practice continued even after the Baillys had title to the grounds.

After Robert was laid to rest, Joseph Bailly erected a large wooden cross, said to be thirty feet high, easily visible to travelers on the Chicago–Detroit Road. He also built a small log building near the site. It had one door, which faced the cross. On Sunday and holy day mornings, as there was no church in the region, the Bailly family would walk to the cemetery, gather in the building, sit quietly, and pray.

Joseph Bailly died in 1835 and was buried in the cemetery. In years to come, Marie and many other family members were buried there as well. In 1866, daughter Rose Bailly Howe (for whom Howe Road is named) tried to restrict the cemetery to Bailly family members only, enclosing the family cemetery with a wooden fence. However, during the five years that her family was in Europe (1869–74), three additional neighbors were buried on the ridge.

As the wooden fence was impermanent, in 1885 Rose had a limestone wall erected. It had an entrance with an iron gate on the south side. Inside were the stations of the cross and an altar. The large wooden cross, erected by her father and by then badly weathered, was replaced by a new one.

By 1914, her daughter Frances, concerned about vandalism, had a concrete block wall built around the old one, had the memorial plaques moved to the wall exteriors, and filled the interior with sand. Frances died in 1918. Hers was the last burial at the site.

The Bailly Homestead and cemetery were within the original boundaries of the National Lakeshore as approved in 1966. The land was purchased and became part of the park in 1971. Two years later, a trail was built connecting the cemetery to the Homestead area.

The Bailly Cemetery atop the Calumet Beach ridge. *Jim Rettker*

## 1833 *The Dream Cities and Daniel Webster*

The mid-1830s was an exciting time throughout the frontier. Beginning in 1832, when the Potawatomi Indians ceded their lands to the federal government, the Calumet Area was opened to speculation and settlement. Many speculators predicted that a huge metropolis would be located on Lake Michigan, and so almost immediately several great cities were planned on or close to the southern Lake Michigan shoreline. John O. Bowers called these the "Dream Cities of the Calumet." Most of these dreams were centered in the Indiana Dunes.

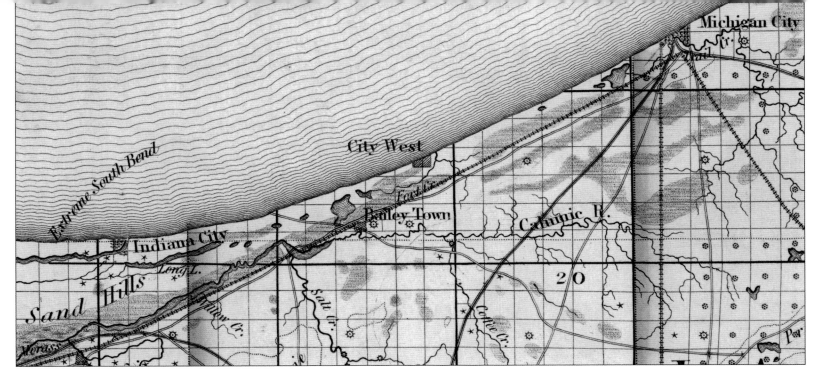

A portion of J. H. Colton's 1838 map of Indiana showing four "dream cities." Also on the map are a railroad and a canal—both proposed, but never built. *Indiana Historical Society*

Daniel Webster, in a daguerreotype taken several years after his 1837 trip to the Midwest.

Michigan City was the first of these dream cities to be platted. When Isaac Elston did that in 1833, he intentionally located the city at the northern end of the almost-finished Michigan Road. Work on the harbor began immediately, but with little immediate funding, improvements came slowly. However, there was enough hope and money to build a lighthouse in 1837.

Town of Bailly (or Bailey Town) was platted in December 1834 by Joseph Bailly about one mile west of his homestead. Unfortunately, he became ill and died twelve months later. Only about five of the 240 lots were ever sold, and the town was never developed.

Waverly (not on the map) was located east of Bailey Town about where Waverly Road crosses Oak Hill Road in Porter. The city was platted in 1835, a few lots were sold, and six log houses, a blacksmith shop, and a factory were built. Elaborate plans were made for a canal to connect the Little Calumet River with Lake Michigan.

Indiana City was to be at the mouth of the Grand Calumet River at what is now Marquette Park in Gary. The city was platted in 1836, but it is doubtful whether any streets or buildings were ever built.

City West, on the other hand, started off with a bang. Located at the mouth of Fort Creek (today Dunes Creek at Dunes State Park), it was platted in 1836 with 1,113 lots. Its investors moved quickly, knowing that Waverly and Michigan City had a head start. To provide lumber, a dam was built across Fort Creek and a sawmill was erected. The town soon had fifteen private homes, a warehouse, and the Exchange Hotel with twenty-two rooms. A small harbor was dug, and trade with Chicago was established.

On July 4, 1837, Senator (and presidential candidate) Daniel Webster visited both City West and Michigan City. He was royally entertained and made patriotic speeches at both cities. His hosts at each city touted the advantages of its location for a federally-funded harbor. But when Webster returned to Washington, he recommended funding only for the Michigan City harbor. The disappointed folks at City West assumed that the promoters of Michigan City had used a higher quality of liquor to entertain the senator on that fateful holiday. The folks at Michigan City would simply have said that theirs was the better location.

A nation-wide financial recession occurred that autumn. Michigan City survived, partially because of the promise of federal funding for its harbor, but Waverly and City West did not. People couldn't pay their bills. Home construction stopped.

Waverly was destroyed by fire in 1838, and by 1840 City West was a ghost town with no residents. It, too, succumbed to fire. Nothing remains now except their names.

- "Bailey Town" still refers to the area around the proposed Town of Bailly (even though it is often spelled differently).
- Waverly Road still exists. The Waverly Schoolhouse was built in 1881. (It closed in 1922 and is now in private hands.) Waverly Beach is the old name for the state park beach.
- City West is the name of one of the picnic shelters at the state park.

## 1833 Michigan City

Michigan City was the first city to be established on the Indiana shoreline of Lake Michigan and the only one of the original "dream cities" to not only survive the financial panic of 1837 but then flourish.

### Two Roads to Permanence

In 1830, Major Isaac Elston purchased land at the mouth of Trail Creek, the proposed north end of the Michigan Road (now Route

Major Isaac Elston. *Daniels, 1904*

35), Indiana's first state "highway." Elston recognized that the road would allow farmers to haul their produce to Michigan City. With a good harbor, the city might become the major Lake Michigan port. Elston recorded his plat of the city in 1833 and began to sell lots. His dream was that this city rather than Chicago would become the great Midwest metropolis. (Chicago then had a population of just 150 persons.) Settlers arrived, houses, hotels, and stores were built, and within two years the population of this new town was 715. (But by then, Chicago had grown to 1,800 persons.)

A second major road was the Chicago–Detroit Road. This east-west route was first used primarily by federal soldiers and mail carriers to get from Detroit to Fort Dearborn and later Chicago. Originally, the route west of the city was simply the Lake Michigan Shoreline. It was sometimes a difficult pathway, but in 1833, stagecoaches began making the trip along that route to Chicago. Michigan City was incorporated as a town in 1836.

The next year, 1837, was eventful for this new city. Not waiting for promised federal support, residents began work on a harbor, but progress was slow. Warehouses were built on land, but boats had to load and unload while anchored out in the lake, and that only during periods of good weather. Nevertheless, Michigan City became the primary grain market for northwest Indiana; in season, it saw up to forty oxcarts of grain arriving every day.

The first lighthouse was built in 1837. Also in that year, the Chicago–Detroit stage route was moved inland to Lake Michigan's ancient Calumet Shoreline (today's Route 12), and stagecoaches began using that more reliable inland route from Michigan City westward. As late as 1862, the Lake House at First and Franklin Streets still advertised that stagecoaches left the house daily for Chicago and Detroit.

## Arrival of the Railroads

The Michigan Central Railroad extended its line to Michigan City in 1850 and established a station and rail yard. By that year, with a population of 996, Michigan City was the largest town in the Calumet Area. Also that year, Congress finally appropriated funds for the development of a harbor, but it was not until about 1870 that the harbor was finished. Even then the city financed

The 1858 lighthouse, now the home of the Old Lighthouse Museum.

HARRIET COLFAX
*Old Lighthouse Museum*

much of the work, especially on Trail Creek, so that the early dream of a good harbor could be realized.

Nevertheless, as more traffic began to use the harbor, a brighter warning light was needed. So, in 1858, a new and larger brick and stone lighthouse was constructed. It had a light visible on clear nights up to fifteen miles away. In 1871, with the new harbor finally completed, a second beacon was established on the east pier. It had a wooden elevated walkway that allowed the lighthouse keeper to get to it even in the worst storms.

But even before the harbor was completed, Michigan City grew. The Monon Railroad arrived in 1853. The Haskell and Barker firm started making railroad cars in Michigan City in 1852, and by 1871 it had made more than fifteen thousand of them. By 1910, it was employing 3,500 employees and producing ten thousand cars a year in its thirty-four buildings. The company was sold to Pullman in 1922 but kept producing through 1971.

Michigan City is in the middle of dune country, and it was at first home to Indiana's largest sand dune. Perhaps two hundred feet high, it was called the Hoosier Slide because of its occasional

One of Michigan City's most noteworthy early citizens was Miss Harriet Colfax, who lived in the old lighthouse building and tended its lights for forty-three years. Miss Colfax, a strong but petite woman, had to maintain the facility, record weather and shipwrecks, and, during the shipping season, physically light the lanterns in the towers every night and extinguish them every morning. The walk out to the beacon on the east pier was often dangerous; more than once, she was nearly swept off the pier by huge waves. She was thirty-seven years old in 1861 when she was offered the position, which then paid $350 a year. She retired in 1904 at the age of eighty.

The Hoosier Slide beside Trail Creek. Note the rail cars next to the shore. *(below) Old Lighthouse Museum*

Franklin Street (circa 1880). Note that the street is paved with wood planks. *(right) Old Lighthouse Museum*

avalanches of sand. Tourists would climb to the top, and there were even weddings conducted up there. As can be seen in the post-card shown here, rail lines were built right up next to the dune so that mining its sand would be easy. By 1920, it was gone; NIPSCO's power plant now is at that site.

The railroads and harbor stimulated growth and prosperity. Huge amounts of timber and grain were shipped into and out of the city. The city modernized. The water works came in 1875, the Gas Light Company arrived in 1881, and in 1886, the Lake Cities Electric Company started supplying electricity—both for residential use and to power Michigan City's streetcars. And, of course, the streets were paved. By the turn of the century, Michigan City had about fifteen thousand residents and a thriving downtown.

Haskell Barker Car Co., Showing City in Rear, Michigan City, Ind.

Colorized Postcard, 1916, *Old Lighthouse Museum*

Indiana State Prison showing the trolley that took employees, visitors, and tourists from the city out to the prison. *Old Lighthouse Museum*

Indiana State Prison entrance colorized postcard (circa 1915). *Old Lighthouse Museum*

## The Indiana State Prison

In 1860, construction began on a new state prison. To recoup its costs and to help pay expenses, the state invited visitors, charging 25¢ for admission.

In 1909, the D Cell House was built. It was five tiers high and contained 340 cells. Well constructed, the building is still in use. The C Cell House was built in 1932 and has 371 cells, making it today the largest in Indiana.

As most folks seem to know, Indiana license plates are made by inmates. That started in 1930 at the same time that its most famous inmate, John Dillinger, was housed there. Dillinger was paroled by the governor in 1933. A few months later, ten inmates escaped—most of them members of Dillinger's gang. Few others have ever escaped from this maximum-security facility.

Another prisoner at that time was Johnson Van Dyke Grigsby, who was sentenced to life imprisonment in 1908 on a second-degree murder charge. He spent sixty-eight years behind bars, and by the time he was paroled in 1976 at age ninety-one, he had been recognized by the Guinness Book of World Records as the country's longest-serving prison inmate. His release was the inspiration for Johnny Cash's song "Michigan City Howdy Do." The song's first stanza ends with the lines:

His old eyes were slowly fadin' as he walked out of the gate.
And he breathed the first free air he'd breathed since 1908.
"Howdy do, Michigan City. You're sure a pretty sight."

Today the Indiana Department of Correction has three local facilities and is the fifth-largest employer in the county.

## A Modern City Emerges

After Washington Park opened in the 1890s, the Lake Erie and Western Railroad encouraged passengers to visit the Duneland playground at Michigan City. Saturday was a big day for $1.50 excursion specials running from Indianapolis. Its fliers advertised boating, bathing, fishing, dune climbing, and even visits to the Indiana State Prison. The LE&W actually owned a "prison car," with iron bars on its windows, that was used to transport felons to the Michigan City Prison. When it was used, it was, of course, always attached to the rear of the train so that passengers wouldn't have to walk through it.

Michigan City matured in the twentieth century. A new lighthouse (correctly called a pierhead light) was built in 1904. The South Shore Railroad was extended into town in 1908. Franklin Street flourished. As railroads grew, the harbor saw fewer cargo ships but fortunately more passenger ships. Washington Park began to bring thousands of visitors from Chicago and other locations. It still does, but they arrive now by automobile or pleasure boat rather than by train or ship. Where excursion ships (including the ill-fated Eastland) used to fill the harbor, three marinas filled with leisure craft now serve the lake-loving public.

The Michigan City Yacht Club was established in 1933, and in 1987 the Club served as host to the Pan American Games yachting events.

Michigan City held its first Miss Indiana pageant in 1957 and since then has hosted forty-two of them, more than any other Indiana city. In 1966, Michigan City was named an "All-America City" by *Look Magazine,* and the Elston High School Red Devils won the state basketball championship. The championship was

The 1904 lighthouse, now the only still-operating lighthouse in Indiana. Years back, the lighthouse keeper had to walk up high along the catwalk whenever the breakwater was covered with ice. *Old Lighthouse Museum*

Trail Creek and Michigan City in 2011 from the Washington Park Observation Tower.

preceded by such an outpouring of community support that a sign in front of St. John's United Church of Christ read, "Contrary to our normal policy, we too are backing the Devils." The victory was noted city-wide by firecrackers, sirens, car horns, and other noisemakers.

By the time of Michigan City's sesquicentennial in 1983, the city recognized itself as a growing sports fishing area, with new marinas for pleasure craft and luxury condominiums sprouting up along the lakefront.

Even though many new residential neighborhoods were being built south and east of the old city, and the primary commercial district had migrated south to Route 20, the city still looked north to the lake and valued its lakefront. The closing of several factories, while disappointing at first, has made opportunities for new development. Lighthouse Place opened on Wabash Street in 1987 and soon became a major destination spot for serious shoppers. The Blue Chip Casino opened in 1997 at its lucky address, 777 Blue Chip Drive. The Lubeznik Center for the Arts opened its new building on Second Street in 2002. The new Senior Center is just steps away from the lake.

Michigan City still looks to Lake Michigan, values Washington Park and its other amenities, and provides numerous opportunities for visitors to enjoy all that it has to offer.

See also: Washington Park, Washington Park Zoo, Fishing, In-Water Boat Show, Great Lakes Grand Prix, and United States Coast Guard

## 1840s Commercial Fishing

Commercial fishing flourished along Duneland's Lake Michigan shoreline for more than a hundred years. The lake had so many fish that the supply must have seemed inexhaustible to the early fishermen.

Although we have no records, commercial fishing must have started as City West and Michigan City were just getting started. Someone undoubtedly went to the lake, caught fish, and sold them to other settlers. In the early days, fishing was done from rowboats or sailboats with "seines"—long homemade nets with weights along their bottom edges and floats along the top. These were rather inefficient but good enough for the limited demand for fish at that time.

Fishing was hard work. Fishermen would leave the shore between two and six AM and usually return in the afternoon. Sometimes they would be out until late at night. When they returned, they had to spread the nets out on the large reels that each family or company owned. The nets often tore, and when that happened they would be repaired by hand.

Fishermen retrieving their catch.
*Calumet Regional Archives*

Whitefish was the principal commercial catch in the early years. Herring was valued in the local Swedish communities but apparently was not a cash product elsewhere. Sturgeon was originally considered a nuisance and discarded, but after 1880 demand for it and the caviar that could be made from it caused it to be so highly valued that it was soon depleted.

## Michigan City

Fishing was big business at Michigan City after 1850 because the rail lines came right up to the port. Freight trains then quickly shipped the fish to Indianapolis, Louisville, and other inland cities. According to E. D. Daniels, in those early years, fourteen thousand pounds of fish could be caught in one day with a single net. On good days, the total fish caught by all the fisheries exceeded a hundred thousand pounds. Daniels noted that sometimes the fisheries couldn't find customers for their huge catch and so fish were discarded. When thousands of folks converged on Michigan City on May 1, 1865, to see the Lincoln funeral train, the guests were fed whitefish.

The fishing crew at Michigan City.
*Old Lighthouse Museum*

However, in 1876, Jasper Packard wrote that the fishing wasn't as good as it used to be. He noted that the best years for catching whitefish were back in 1856 and 1857.

Many families were engaged in the Michigan City fisheries. Peter Johnson owned a steam-powered tub and a large sailboat, and he had eight employees. Several of the fishing families became wealthy. But those who continued in the business into the twentieth century lost much of their investment. Mr. Daniels in 1904 noted that the whitefish catch no longer reached two thousand pounds even in an entire year. He assumed that sewage dumped into the lake drove the fish away. Or perhaps, he noted, so many fish had been caught that the supply was simply exhausted.

## Miller Beach

Nobody knows when commercial fishing first began at Miller Beach because the fishing families in that remote area seldom bothered to purchase the land where they lived and worked. When William and Carolina Carr settled on the lakefront with their family in 1862, there had been other fishermen there already. However,

DRUSILLA CARR
*Lake Street Gallery*

ACCORDING TO DRUSILLA:

My husband was a fisherman and fished for whitefish and sturgeon. [At first] we could trade them for flour, buckwheat, pork, butter and so forth with the local farmers who would come down to our place on the lake.

Finally . . . a man from South Chicago . . . wanted to buy our sturgeon if we would take them over.

I always helped do the fishing. When my oldest son was a baby, I took him with me and rolled him up in a blanket and laid him on the beach. As we moved our windlasses closer together, I moved the baby accordingly.

We had a sailboat and on one particular night my husband had gone to South Chicago with a load of sturgeon and was late coming back. I was sitting out on the doorstep waiting to see if I could see a sail anywhere on the lake.

the only other residents on the beach at the time of their arrival were Allen Dutcher, a boat builder from Michigan City, John (Jacques) Beaubien, a trapper from Chicago, and an older man known both as "Colonel" and Davy Crockett, a fugitive slave from the South. Crockett's home, a log shanty at the old mouth of the Calumet River, was the oldest house on the beach.

Sixteen-year-old Drusilla Benn came to the beach in 1872 to live with a brother and cook for fishermen John and Hank Granger. Two years later, she married the Carrs' son Robert. That same year, the B&O Railroad opened a depot in Miller, so the Carrs began carting much of their fish to the depot for shipment to Chicago.

Drusilla Carr befriended Octave Chanute during the summer of 1896, becoming one of his staunch defenders against fellow townsmen who called Chanute the "Crazy Old Man of the Sand Dunes" and spread fables that his glider wings were thatched with chicken feathers.

The Carrs were "squatters" and never did purchase their beach property. When they found it, it was unwanted by others. No one seemed to care that they were there—that is, until US Steel wanted

Gil, Fred, and Hank drying their fishnets. Fred and Hank may be Robert and Drusilla's sons. *Courtesy of Jean Graham Buckley*

The morning catch at Carr's Beach.
*Lake Street Gallery*

the land in 1908. By that time, the Carrs had been there for forty-four years and maintained that they had a legal right to remain. However, US Steel had purchased and even paid back taxes on the land. After legal battles lasting more than thirty years, the Carrs had to give up most of the property—keeping their home, some acreage, and the right to fish. When Drusilla died, Rev. Backemeyer of Gary's First Presbyterian Church praised her by saying, "She was a heroic little soul who stood her ground when she thought she was in the right. Strength, courage, and dignity were her clothing."

## Waverly and Porter Beaches

The Johnson family fished at Waverly and Porter Beaches from 1907 when John "Fish" Johnson arrived until 1952 when his sons retired. Fish was a Swede who came to the Baileytown area in 1869. He worked for a while at one of the Porter brickyards and then sold his farm and went to the lake to fish. Fish and his wife had fourteen children.

The Johnsons originally fished where Porter Beach is today but soon moved their operations east to Waverly Beach (where

As I sat . . . I saw [sturgeon] jumping. I thought, *My, what a haul we could make if some one was only here to help me.* "Colonel" Crockett went out and found help. The men went out in the boat and laid the seine [fishing net]. I picked up driftwood and made two fires--one where they went out and the other to come in by. We pulled in the net and wound up the windlasses . . . and had 57 large sturgeon. About the time we had them lined up, the boat containing my husband and his men came in from South Chicago, and there we had another load ready to go. They were surprised.

———

There were lots of white and blue cranes, and hundreds of bald eagles along the beach. When we went along the lake we could see an eagle on every hill, but we don't see any more. . . . Once I was attacked by one and had a terrible time with it . . . when I went down to the beach, it tried to get at my baby. The eagle was terribly hungry and I fought with it for quite a while. My sunbonnet seemed to keep it away from my head and eyes, but I had to fight hard to keep it away; and it might have gotten the baby if it hadn't been for the bonnet. My husband was out in the lake in a boat looking after the nets, and when he heard me call, he came in and used his paddle on the bird and drove it off.

—DRUSILLA CARR, 1921, Miller Station

the state park pavilion is now). "Fish" and his sons hauled their catch to Porter and Chesterton, where they traversed the streets calling out "fresh fish." They used a two-masted sailboat to drop their nets. They also had an icehouse filled with about a hundred tons of ice, harvested the previous winter, to keep their fish fresh. When Prairie Club members and later local residents started coming to the lake for hikes and summer swims, the Johnsons sold fish lunches and rented boats and bathing suits to make some extra money. The Johnsons then established a great restaurant that specialized in fried perch dinners. Just imagine: Fish, potatoes, salad, veggies, and bread and butter for just one dollar.

Meanwhile, back at the Porter Beach location, Dick Sabinske started fishing. Like the Johnsons, Sabinske hauled fish to Chesterton and Porter and also sold some to fish stores in Gary and Michigan City.

When the state purchased Waverly Beach for the new state park, Fish's sons Will and Elmer, who had inherited the business, moved back to Porter Beach. There they built a new fish house and the multi-story Johnson's Inn. They paved Wabash Street and had an electric line extended north to their buildings. Their land was soon known as Johnson's Beach.

The inn opened in 1930 with a grill and grocery on the ground floor, a dining room seating a hundred on the second floor, and fifteen small rooms for guests on the third. In addition to fishing, Dick Sabinske and the Johnsons should be given credit for saving a lot of people from drowning during their years on the beach.

More fish were caught in one day in the early years than by 1950. By then, a hundred pounds a day was a good catch. The Johnson brothers' families operated their restaurant and fishing business until 1952, when they retired.

## A Real Fish Story

In June, 1912, the Johnsons caught a 9'11½" sturgeon that weighed 235 pounds—the largest sturgeon ever caught on the south shore. It sold for $63 and yielded thirty-eight pounds of caviar.

Postcard of Waverly Beach (where Dunes State Park's pavilion is today), postmarked August 4, 1927. Note the boat, diamond-shaped net drying rack, and windlass on the beach and the Devil's Slide (dune) at the far right. *(above) Calumet Regional Archives*

July 27, 1916 ad for Johnson's restaurant. *(below) Westchester Township History Museum*

The Fish House (left) and
Johnson's Inn at Porter Beach, 1936.
*Calumet Regional Archives*

## The Decline

Many factors caused the fish population to change drastically over
the last 150 years. The decline started in the early years of settlement, when dams were placed across many of the lake's tributaries,
which fish used for spawning. The dumping of sawdust from sawmills often then despoiled the streams downstream. Overfishing,
chemical pollution, and untreated sewage obviously played large
parts in later years. Another factor was the accidental introduction
of exotic species into the lake.

Nearly two hundred non-native species have invaded the waters
of the Great Lakes since the early 1800s, and many of these have
become permanent residents of Lake Michigan. These successful exotics often had detrimental effects on native species. Among
these aliens are the sea lamprey, alewife, and zebra mussel.

According to the Great Lakes Fishery Commission, sea lampreys
were a major cause of the collapse of lake trout, whitefish, and chub
populations in the Great Lakes during the 1940s and 1950s. The
commission's control efforts have reduced the lamprey population
by 90 percent, but total eradication is probably impossible.

Perch has for years been a favorite catch from the lake. However, commercial fishing for yellow perch in Indiana, Illinois, and
Wisconsin was halted in 1997 as a result of sudden and dramatic

population collapse. Unfortunately, even with the ban, the perch population has not significantly rebounded. Today, there is no commercial fishing on Indiana's portion of Lake Michigan.

Sport fishing, however, is alive and well.

# 1851 Miller

Just as Michigan City is the urban anchor near the east end of Duneland, Gary's Miller Beach community is the urban anchor at the west end—and has been so for about 150 years.

## Early Settlements

At some time between 1844 and 1850, Samuel and Susan Miller are believed to have opened an inn on the stagecoach road that ran south of today's Route 12.

If so, then travelers going to Chicago could have spent the night at Miller's Inn before heading farther west the next day. Samuel and Susan had at least five children, one of whom, three-year-old John S. Miller, died in 1850. His was the first known burial in what is now known as the Miller Cemetery.

## Arrival of the Railroads

The Northern Indiana Railroad (later the Michigan Southern and Northern Indiana) was the first of several railroads to run its tracks through Miller. In 1851, its tracks were laid parallel to, but north of, where Miller Avenue is today.

The railroad didn't build a depot—at least, not right away. However, Timothy Ball reported that there was one by 1872. Nevertheless, the railroad, with its new passenger service, helped put many stagecoach lines out of business and most likely caused the Miller family to close its inn. According to various stories about the early town, Samuel Miller then worked for the railroad providing wood (for fuel) and water, keeping the roadbed in good condition, and building the station house. When the railroad (by then renamed the Lake Shore and Michigan Southern) opened a station, it was called "Miller's Station." The Miller family, however, didn't remain in the area for long. With the inn apparently closed, the family headed off to begin anew in the far west, leaving its name behind.

Miller's Station in 1872 was a village with twelve families, a little grocery store, a schoolhouse, and a railroad station. The station was used to ship ice from Long Lake to customers in Chicago and other cities. A gravel road ran from Miller to the little community of Hobart. Today it's still called the Hobart Road.

The Baltimore and Ohio Railroad laid its rail line through town in 1874, crossing the Lake Shore and Michigan Southern tracks at what is today Lake Street. The B&O built a depot west of Lake Street and almost immediately began to play an important part in Miller's economy. Two sand mining companies purchased land near the depot and started the quite profitable mining of sand. (The Santa Fe Railroad is said to have placed an order in 1899 for 150,000 cars of sand to be obtained from the Miller area.)

In July, 1875, William Ewing platted the first subdivision of the town, which he also called "Miller's Station." Four years later, the Miller's Station post office opened. The town changed its name

The intersection of the B&O and Lake Shore Railroads at Miller's Station, 1889. The track running from the center of the photo to the lower right corner was the Lake Shore line (earlier the Michigan Southern and Northern Indiana). It ran parallel to today's Miller Avenue. The B&O line enters the photo on the bottom left. Stationmaster W. J. Cook is standing at the track intersection. *Courtesy of Jean Graham Buckley*

Miller's first brick school building, built around 1890 and used until 1909. The building in the background to the right is the older frame primary school building. *Courtesy of Jean Graham Buckley*

"Miller" in 1882. By then, Miller and the surrounding area had begun to attract a large number of Swedish immigrants, and in a short time Miller became known informally as a Swedish village.

Residents found jobs cutting wood for the railroads (which had wood-burning locomotives), mining sand, and cutting ice in the winter. After 1881, jobs were also available at the nearby Aetna Powder Works. The first church in town was the Swedish (now Bethel) Lutheran Church, established in 1874. Its first structure was built on Lake Street in 1894 and still stands there. Until 1905, all services were conducted in the Swedish language with the men seated on one side and women on the other. That tradition apparently ended when one obstinate woman shocked the congregation by sitting next to her husband. With the tradition broken, others did the same.

At the turn of the century, the village of Miller had a population of about eighty, a general store, one church, two school buildings, and two saloons. The son of the store's owner, Charles Blank, wrote in his diary that Miller was then "wild and wide-open" and that a restraining hand was "imperative."

## Industrial "Suburb" and Beach Town

In 1906, US Steel started building what would become the world's largest steel mill, and Gary was established as a town. That year, Miller residents were startled to hear that the Gary town board, at its first meeting, annexed the Clarke and Buffington areas west of the new town. Accordingly, the citizens of Miller united, and in 1907, Miller was incorporated as an independent town. Three years later, its first census listed 638 residents.

In spite of its independent status, Miller was about to change. In 1908, the South Shore Railroad line was built, and a station was constructed at Miller. The town's growth accelerated. One could now live in Miller and work at the steel mills in Gary. In 1910, a new, handsome brick school was built (and still stands) on Lake Street. (Students who wanted to attend high school still had to go to Hobart.) By 1911, the town had enough funding to build a town hall, also still standing at the corner of Miller Avenue and Grand Boulevard.

The wooden Lake Street bridge over the Grand Calumet River. According to Hanna Westergren, "The water used to be real deep by the bridge and we did all our swimming there until the lake warmed up in the summer. A big game for the boys was diving for pennies . . . under the bridge." *(below left) Calumet Regional Archives*

Miller Town Hall when new. (Postcard with a 1915 postmark.) Used for many years as a fire station after annexation by the City of Gary. (below) *Courtesy of Jean Graham Buckley*

## Miller Beach

As Gary grew, its residents started coming out to the beach for a swim. Even though there was no road, summers in the city were hot enough that folks would walk the one and a half miles from the train station to the lake. Lakeshore residents Drusilla Carr and her sons then opened a bathhouse at the beach where they rented bathing suits and sold refreshments. They soon discovered that catering to bathers could provide a nice supplement to their fishing income.

According to Steve Spicer, Carr's Beach was a vibrant playland with a miniature railroad, a shooting gallery, a pleasure boat, and several night spots. Fred Carr, Robert and Drusilla's son, managed a dance hall and roller rink. The Carrs also, for $100 a year, rented space on their "property," where folks built private cottages.

The city planners of Gary wanted parkland along the beach. So in 1918, Gary annexed Miller. Once it was part of Gary, Miller grew rapidly. There was now money for improvements, such as paving streets and sidewalks. Lake Street became the center of a thriving business community.

## Marquette Park

Marquette Park was the dream of William P. Gleason, superintendent of US Steel's Gary Works and president of both the National Dunes Park Association and the Gary Park Board.

Gary in 1910 was a brand-new, growing city with the world's largest steel mill and already more than sixteen thousand residents. Although on the lake, it had no public lakefront. So after Gary annexed Miller, Gleason convinced the company to purchase land for the park from its various owners and donate those 120 acres to the city.

The wild dune and swale landscape was smoothed out and transformed into a true destination location: Lake Front Park. Thickets and underbrush were removed, as were several of the dune ridges, so that the circular roadway and extensive picnic groves could be built.

The Park's bathhouse had changing areas for men and women, with 2,200 lockers and 5,000 bathing suits to rent to bathers. The Pavilion, with its restaurant and banquet hall, was opened

Carr's dance pavilion at the foot of Lake Street, July 4, 1917. *Calumet Regional Archives*

The Gary Bathhouse, now the Aquatorium. *Lake Street Gallery*

The Gay Mill on North Lake Street.
*Calumet Regional Archives*

WORKING AT THE GAY MILL
I was on the staff at Gay Mill and there were five other girls. Our job was to be a hostess and take tickets for each dance. We girls were not supposed to accept any dances while on the job but it became very hard sometimes to stick to the rules.

Our uniforms were not at all like what you would see your modern day hostess in. All six of us girls were outfitted in white satin dresses and white felt tams. I guess you could say we looked like the "cat's meow."

I don't want to forget to tell you about our boss or the host at Gay Mill. He was what is now known as a bouncer. The thing that was watched closely in our place was that couples didn't dance too close together. The forbidden dance then was the "shimmy." I suppose it did look a little immoral, but it sure was fun to get out there and really wiggle!

—LILLIAN WESTERGREN WEIGER;
transcribed by Denise Ramirez

to the public in 1923. In the years since, it has been used for thousands of high school proms, wedding receptions, and cultural association banquets. And in 1930, a bronze statue of Father Jacques Marquette was placed at the park entrance as it was renamed in Marquette's honor.

## The Roaring Twenties

One of the many new businesses in town in the 1920s was the Gay Mill, a vibrant dance and social hall with an adjacent hotel and even lakefront houses for rent. Opened in 1922 or 1923 and run by Thomas J. Johnson, it was located on Lake Street just south of the Calumet River bridge. The place had dance bands that played all the popular music of the time. Many folks came by way of the South Shore Railroad to join the fun, some from as far away as Chicago. The Gay Mill was the place to be on Saturday— or just about any other night.

Business dropped off during the Great Depression, and when the building burned down in 1935, it was not rebuilt.

## The Modern Community

After the 1920s, Miller matured as a community. St. Mary of the Lake Catholic Church was established in 1931, followed by churches of many other denominations. Wirt High School was built in 1938. The Wildermuth branch of the Gary Public Library opened in 1954. In the postwar era, Miller's population surpassed seventeen thousand residents. Rather than tearing down the dunes first, many houses were by then being built on the dunes themselves. Miller quickly became Gary's most affluent neighborhood. Its larger lots and proximity to the lake were its primary attractions.

As it did in 1915, Miller today still welcomes visitors to its beach. In 2010, Gary received a 28-million-dollar grant to refurbish Marquette Park giving the entire park, its buildings, its open lands, and even Father Marquette a fresh new look.

## 1853 Furnessville

Furnessville is an unincorporated community alongside Furnessville Road and US Route 20. The first home was built in 1853 by the
Morgan family, just two years after the Michigan Central Railroad
came through. Edwin and Louise Furness built a home in 1855
and opened a store in their basement. They joined forces with the
Morgans and established the lumbering firm of Morgan, Furness,
and Co. The lumber business was an important industry with as
many as three sawmills operating at one time. Morgan's Side Track
became the name of what was one of the Calumet Area's first local
railroads, one with wooden rails and "trains" drawn by horses or
mules. The Michigan Central established a depot with Edwin Furness serving as the first station agent. In 1861, he became the first
"Furnessville" postmaster.

Furnessville took on an English flavor when a number of families
including the Brummitts, Paynes, and Teales arrived from York-
shire. In 1929, the Dunes Relief Highway (Route 20) cut through
the middle of this rural community and forced the removal of
several nineteenth-century farm houses. Soon, students from the
School of the Art Institute of Chicago found homes in the area,
giving Furnessville the aura of an arts colony. Much of this historic
community north of Route 20 is now within the National Lakeshore.

## 1855 Sand Mining

Sand is a commercially valuable natural resource. It is an excellent
material to use when highways, railroads, or parkland need to be
elevated because it settles quickly and remains stationary as long as
it is protected from wind or flowing water. Sand is also used in the
manufacture of glass. It can even be used to make bricks. Michigan City once had a factory that used sand for making sand-lime
bricks. Not surprisingly, the mining of sand in northwest Indiana
became big business.

Using horse and manpower to remove sand (circa 1908). *Ed Hedstrom South Shore Collection*

Dumping sand from rail cars to raise the grade level (circa 1908). *Ed Hedstrom South Shore Collection*

Clean Drift LAKE MICHIGAN~Core Sand

Advertisement for clean sand. *NPS*

Mining sand was also relatively simple. With a rail spur built alongside a dune, the chore typically required just three men; a crane operator and two helpers could load from ten to fifteen rail cars a day.

Sand mining was possible on a commercial scale as soon as the railroads arrived. In fact, the first major sand mining of the dunes was done either to remove a dune that was "in the way" of a new rail line or to provide material for railroad embankments.

After the Chicago Fire of 1871, Chicago decided to expand its lakefront area by building eastward into the lake. To do so required vast amounts of material to dump into Lake Michigan. Much of the fill obtained was Indiana sand. Sand was also carted off to make glass at several Central Indiana factories, to beautify sand-less resort lakes, and to build up railroad rights of way.

By the 1890s, the mining and exporting of sand was big business at the railroad stations at Miller, Dune Park, and Michigan City. Because of the hauling of dune sand, the Dune Park Station became the most profitable station on the Lake Shore Railroad between Elkhart and Chicago.

An alternative way of mining sand that did not require railroad spurs, permission, or even payment was sucking wet sand up from the bottom of the lake. To do this, steamships with large cargo spaces were fitted with sand-sucking equipment and sent out to the south shore of the lake. The *Muskegon* and the *J. D. Marshall* were both sandsuckers. Today they lie on top of the sand they once harvested at the bottom of Lake Michigan.

Hoosier Slide and railroad yard. *Old Lighthouse Museum*

In 1928, George Cressey reported that near Dunes State Park there was nearly a square mile of land where the dunes had been removed and sent to Chicago.

The Hoosier Slide was once said to be Indiana's largest sand dune. It used to be at Michigan City where Trail Creek entered Lake Michigan. This enormous dune was nearly two hundred feet high, much taller than Mt. Tom is today. In 1900, Timothy Ball noted that "immense quantities" of sand had already been removed, but that it was "a huge mass yet."

By 1920, it was all gone. The NIPSCO power station now sits on the site of what was once said to be the greatest sand dune in the country. By 1912, concerned citizens feared that the entire Duneland area would be stripped of its dunes, and so the "Save the Dunes" movement slowly began. Yet for the next sixty years, sand mining continued.

As late as 1952, the Indiana Geological Survey reported that five thousand tons of sand were still being removed daily from a total of ten large sand pits and several smaller ones, all less than three miles from the lake. The report noted that large tracts "once comprising some of the most spectacular and picturesque dunes already have been cleared of sand." According to the authors, this was good: "After the sands have been removed, the property may be prepared for subdividing." They added, "because of the many problems of building on sand dunes, the average householder probably will be better satisfied to live on the more level ground of the worked-out sand area." The report concluded that few large reserves of sand were still available to the sand industry, but that if the present conditions and demand were maintained, perhaps fifty to a hundred years of sand operations would still be possible.

Illinois geologist J. Harlan Bretz noted in 1955 that whenever Chicago needed sand for fill, it got it from the "inexhaustible supplies heaped up in the dunes along the nearby Indiana lakeshore."

## 1865 Abraham Lincoln's Duneland Funeral

Abraham Lincoln, 1865. Taken two months before his assassination, this photograph of the president shows the weariness and strain caused by four years of civil war. *Alexander Gardner*

Abraham Lincoln was assassinated in Washington, D.C., on April 14, 1865. When Mrs. Lincoln decided that she wanted him buried at Springfield, Illinois, his body was taken by train from Washington to Springfield—but not in a direct route. Instead, the funeral train took an indirect route that went through 180 cities. The coffin was taken off of the train and funeral services held in nine of these cities, including New York, Indianapolis, and Chicago.

At midnight on the morning of May 1, the train left downtown Indianapolis. Bonfires and torches lit the route as it headed north. Arriving at Lafayette at 3:35 A M, the train moved through the city at five miles an hour to the tolling of church bells and a funeral dirge played by a band. As elsewhere along the route, men removed their hats, and all stood in respectful silence for Indiana's favorite son. (He had, after all, grown up in Indiana.) Many wept.

Heading north on the Monon tracks, the train passed through Medaryville at dawn and began the last leg of its journey to Michigan City. Historian E. D. Daniels wrote that great preparations were made at Michigan City to solemnly welcome the train. As in many other cities, citizen volunteers had built a large memorial arch over the tracks containing patriotic statements and black mourning ribbons.

Michigan City residents, under their lovingly-made funeral arch, quietly wait for the arrival of the funeral train bearing the body of assassinated President Abraham Lincoln. The city was numbed earlier by the news of the president's assassination, coming just five days after the celebration of Robert E. Lee's surrender at Appomattox Courthouse. *Bill Warrick*

The train arrived at about 8:00 AM. There it had to switch to the Michigan Central tracks for its trip through Duneland and onward to Chicago.

A number of young girls led by Harriet Colfax, all in long black skirts, were permitted to enter the car that contained the remains of the President and lay a floral cross on the casket. Daniels noted that the flowers included trailing arbutus, which Harriet had gathered from the hills around the city.

Meanwhile, the three hundred passengers on the funeral train were escorted into the freshly scrubbed freight depot. There they were given a whitefish breakfast that had been lovingly prepared by the ladies of the city, who had set the tables with their best linen and silver.

It was soon discovered, however, that the train's departure had to be delayed because a contingent of about a hundred prominent Chicagoans, who had permission to ride the funeral train into that city, had not yet arrived.

Plans were quickly changed. Military officials aboard the train decided on the spot that President Lincoln's coffin could be opened, and local citizens were permitted to board the train and pay their respects. Clergy who were present conducted an impromptu thirty-five-minute funeral service. Hymns were sung, and a girl's choir sang patriotic songs. After the brief service and the breakfast were finished, the passengers reboarded, and the funeral train took off, passing through Porter and Lake Station on its way to the next scheduled funeral in Chicago.

## 1869 *The Chellberg Farm*

Anders and Johanna Kjellberg and their son Cahrl Lewis were all born in Sweden and came to Baillytown in 1863, when Cahrl was four years old. According to family stories, Anders was hired by the Bailly's son-in-law Joel Wicker to "clean out the brush and get the land ready for planting." Wicker gave the Kjellbergs the use of a log house until they could save up enough money to purchase their own home. Anders and Johanna purchased their eighty-acre farm in 1869.

The barn, a frame house, and of course the outhouse were built first. The house now standing on the property, made of brick from the nearby Porter brickyards, was built in 1885 after the first one burned down. Other structures were a granary, chicken coop, corn crib, shed, smokehouse, and pumphouse, perhaps with a windmill. In 1879 the farm was described as having forty acres of tilled land, twenty acres of pasture and/or orchard, ten acres of woods, and ten acres unimproved.

The Kjellbergs were one of a large number of Swedish families that settled in northern Lake and Porter Counties around the 1860s and 1870s. Soon Hobart, Miller, Porter, and Chesterton all

The Chellberg farmhouse, 1908, with C. L. and Mina Chellberg, daughters Ruth and Naomi, and the family dog. *NPS*

had Swedish churches. Anders had been a lay preacher in Sweden. Once established in the Baillytown area, he and Johanna joined the Augsburg Lutheran Church in Porter. Besides their faith, these immigrants brought with them their love of Swedish customs and foods.

Cahrl (called C. L.) and his sister Emily and her husband took over management of the farm in 1887. Around this time, he anglicized his name to Carl Chellberg. In 1901, at the age of forty-two, he married OttoMina (Mina) Peterson. Mina tended the gardens. Besides her flower garden, she had a kitchen garden where she planted vegetables, raspberries, and herbs. In 1908, C. L. started a dairy farm. Every morning he carted fresh milk to the new South Shore depot, where it was then taken to an East Chicago dairy.

Santa Lucia Day and Christmas were important holidays in most Swedish American families, and that certainly included the Chellbergs. Mina started preparations early by baking cookies. Limpa (rye) bread, sweet rolls, sponge cake, fruit soup, potato sausage, meatballs, and lutefisk were all made later. But Santa Lucia Day came first.

On Santa Lucia Day, December 13, either Ruth or Naomi would wake early, dress in white, and, wearing a green wreath with seven candles on her head, wake her parents and serve them coffee and Santa Lucia buns in bed. Traditionally, the candles would have been lighted, but Naomi admitted years later that she was afraid of fire and that unlighted candles were good enough for her.

On Christmas Eve, the family would have a traditional Swedish smörgåsbord, open gifts, go to bed early, and then wake at four AM to be at church in Porter for a special five o'clock "Julotta" Christmas service.

Midsummer, June 23 or 24, was also celebrated by the Chellbergs. With Scandinavian summers being so short, the longest day of the year was a time to celebrate. Festivities included raising a maypole, singing, and dancing with family and neighbors.

Apparently, C. L. was quite interested in learning the best ways to improve his farming techniques. After the house was purchased by the National Park Service, a number of USDA Farmer's Bulletins from 1896–1908 were found in the home. Mina was said to have been an excellent cook. Besides cooking for the family, she catered parties in the 1920s at the nearby Dune Acres Country Club. In

Chellberg Farm, circa 1922. *NPS*

1919, the house and barn were electrified—but with batteries and generators that were stored on the side porch.

Times were tough during the Great Depression, and to help pay the family's taxes, C. L started making and selling maple syrup. In 1934 he had a "Maple Sugar Camp" built where sap from more than a hundred sugar maple trees was collected and boiled in large evaporation pans. Sap collection began in January when the temperature went above freezing and continued through early March. The family made up to sixty gallons of syrup each year. Syrup in those years could fetch between four and ten dollars a gallon.

C. L. Chellberg died in 1937, and his son Carl assumed operation of the farm. Under Carl's ownership, things changed. He stopped threshing and started raising sheep. In the mid-fifties, he sold the sheep and got a job at a Chesterton machine shop while his wife Hilda started working as a cook at a local restaurant. Farming was no longer the family's main business.

In 1972, Carl and family sold the farm to the National Park Service. In the years since, the house, barn, and outbuildings have been repaired and opened to the public.

The property was representative of farms in the local Swedish community. And so for years the National Lakeshore managed the property as a working farm and established an active interpretation program that reflected its heritage. The farm is now the site of the annual Maple Sugar Time program.

Angel Gochee of Porter, a volunteer at both the Indiana Dunes National Lakeshore and Indiana Dunes State Park, in the kitchen at the Chellberg Farm. Angel was named the 2002 national "Outstanding Interpretive Volunteer of the Year" by the National Association for Interpretation. *(left) Cliff Goins*

A volunteer uses a disk harrow to prepare the soil for planting at the Chellberg Farm. *(below) Michael Kobe*

*See also: Maple Sugar Time, Midsummer, and Santa Lucia Festival*

# 1881 Explosions in the Dunes

Perhaps the most unusual company to find a home in the dunes was the Aetna Powder Works.

In 1881, the Miami Powder Company chose the Indiana Dunes as the location for its newest powder plant because the high, unpopulated dunes were perfect buffers for a factory that might explode at any minute. Explosions did occur, and on occasion they would crack the walls of the Miller schoolhouse. Whenever that happened, the students went home early to find out whether the explosion had injured their fathers or brothers.

Between 1881 and 1888, the company purchased more than nine hundred acres about 11/4 miles southwest of Miller. In short time, the company had twenty-six buildings, employed forty-five men, and was producing sixty thousand pounds of powder a day. Until the Wabash Railroad was built in 1895, the powder made at the plant had to be hauled to the B&O depot in Miller.

According to historian Powell Moore, regional farmers were encouraged to buy the powder because when clearing land for farming, it was easier to blow tree stumps to smithereens than to manually hack them up.

The company buildings were arranged to have a sand dune or ridge between them so that there would be minimum damage when an explosion did occur. All this was a good thing, because occur they did! One day, more than twenty employees of the plant were buried in a single grave in the Miller cemetery. The following headline is from the Chesterton Tribune on April 12, 1888.

James Graham transporting gunpowder in a powder truck by horse-drawn rail, 1895. *Courtesy of Jean Graham Buckley*

## TERRIBLE EXPLOSION

3,000 Pounds of Nitro-glycerin Accidentally Explodes at the Aetna Powder Works. Three Men Blown Into Atoms and Parts of Their Bodies Found a Mile Away.

The article stated that the explosion was heard in Fort Wayne. It went on to say that "the building was blown up and broken into kindling wood, iron pipes . . . were twisted into knots, and the tanks wrenched into all sorts of shapes."

The Aetna Powder Works boiler house alongside the Wabash Railroad tracks, 1915.
*Courtesy of Jean Graham Buckley*

In spite of the dangers, men looking for jobs continued to sign up for employment. Just before World War I, the plant employed about three hundred workers, many of whom lived near the plant. Others lived in Miller, Tolleston, or (after 1906) Gary. The company had a clubhouse where employees could find newspapers, books, and magazines. Alcohol was prohibited.

The town of Aetna was developed around the plant. But because of the dangerous environment, there were no churches, and only one store owner was willing to set up shop in town. Aetna was incorporated as a town in 1907, apparently to insure its independence and prevent annexation and control by the new city of Gary.

In 1912, an explosion of eight hundred pounds of dynamite killed six employees. The tragedy could have been much worse if it had occurred a few minutes later when a crowded South Shore train was to have passed by. Two years later, two thousand pounds of nitroglycerine exploded, which resulted in a vibrant shaking of the ground as far away as downtown Gary where, it was said, every store window on Broadway (between Fourth and Fifth Avenues) was shattered.

Citizens and government officials called for the plant to be closed, but the demands of World War I ensured its continuation for another four years. Employment peaked during the war when close to 1,200 men were employed in the manufacture of gun cotton. The plant at that time was guarded by soldiers to protect it from sabotage. However, after the war, the plant closed its doors for good.

The city of Gary annexed Aetna in 1924. The first subdivision was then platted two years later, and Aetna became a Gary neighborhood. However, about thirty-five years later, Aetna neighborhood children found some nitrated gun-cotton buried by sand and put matches to it. The gun-cotton exploded, injuring two of them.

## 1889 *The United States Coast Guard*

In 1882, Congress authorized a Life Saving Service unit to be established on the Lake Michigan shore east of Trail Creek. Operations began in 1889. The station crew originally consisted of six civilians, called surfmen, commanded by a military officer called a keeper (better known, at least in Michigan City, as "Captain"). It was the keeper's job to keep accurate records and to ensure that his men had constant training. He resided on base year-round. The surf-men were only on duty during the active season, from April to December.

By their own accounts, life at the station was rather dull most of the time. Occasionally there would be moments of "high adventure" as a ship, sailors, or passengers needed to be saved during a major storm. The surfmen and their keeper were "first responders" who on occasion performed their duties at great personal risk. In the early days, of course, the rescue boats had no motors and had to be rowed through often high and dangerous lake waves to get to vessels in serious trouble.

High-tech equipment in those days consisted of a Lyle gun that could shoot a small projectile to a stranded ship up to six hundred yards away. The projectile had a light line that stranded sailors could use to pull a towline out to their boat.

After 1908, the Service purchased gasoline-powered boats for their rescue operations. Greatly appreciated by the men, the new boats didn't lessen the danger of operations, but no longer were the rescuers exhausted by just rowing their rescue boats (usually in rough waters) to the scene of a disaster.

In 1915, the Life Saving Service became part of the United States Coast Guard. Keepers became warrant officers. Number one surfmen became petty officers, while the other surfmen were enlisted men.

Station Michigan City, Indiana's only Coast Guard unit, patrols an area extending north to the harbor at New Buffalo, Michigan. As in the early days, the station is still involved in search and rescue missions, but it also works in maritime law enforcement, security, and marine environmental protection. Safety inspections of recreational boats ensure that they have all federally-required safety equipment aboard. Occasional law enforcement boardings primarily focus on recreational boating safety and enforcement of laws against boating while intoxicated.

Postcard of a life-saving drill (before 1915) at the US Life Saving Station at Washington Park. *Old Lighthouse Museum*

U. S. Life Saving Station Crew at Drill
Michigan City, Ind.

After the attacks of September 11, 2001, Station Michigan City began handling the security of ports, waterways, and coasts. This new duty includes regular security patrols along the Indiana and Michigan lakeshore to protect against potential sabotage. In March, 2003, the Coast Guard became part of the US Department of Homeland Security so as to streamline and improve the focus of these proactive protection activities. The crew today consists of nineteen enlisted active-duty members and seven members of the Coast Guard Reserve. Its largest vessel is a 47' boat that can endure 30' waves and, if capsized, right itself within a few seconds.

The city of Michigan City has always considered itself fortunate to have this federal service right at the tip of its harbor.

Station Michigan City's 47' lifeboat. *US Coast Guard*

## 1890 Washington Park

Martin Krueger. *Old Lighthouse Museum*

Washington Park was the dream, and is now the legacy, of six-term Michigan City mayor Martin T. Krueger. The city's lakefront was a wasteland when Krueger was first elected mayor in 1888. Commercial fishing and shipping were in decline. Yet selling the idea of a lakefront park was not easy, and for access to the site the city would have to build a bridge across Trail Creek. At that time, there were no parks along the Lake Michigan shoreline in Indiana. This one would be the first.

Today, Washington Park is so well-used and in such a perfect location that it is hard to imagine the opposition that arose to Krueger's idea. The bridge would be too expensive; it would harm navigation; it would be a "bridge to nowhere."

Evidently, Mayor Krueger was as persistent as he was persuasive. In 1890, he succeeded in getting some county money and bonds approved to pay for the bridge. In 1891, a new state law allowed cities and towns to create and to levy taxes for public parks. Fortunately, the editors of the *Michigan City Dispatch* supported him. The bridge was built, land was acquired, and every citizen was asked to provide a tree. The park was born.

Park amenities were added as attendance grew. Soon there were a bathhouse, a baseball diamond, a water slide, and a dance hall. Perhaps the most famous attraction was the amusement park with its carousel and roller coaster. Soon excursion boats from Lake County and Chicago started arriving, bringing thousands of visitors to the park for weekend jaunts. A bandstand was built for outdoor concerts while the Oasis Ballroom drew crowds for its dances with big-name bands. There was even a narrow-gauge train to help folks get around.

Michigan City had become a tourist destination. Side trips included climbing the Hoosier Slide (or getting married at its summit), renting boats or going on cruises, or visiting the state prison (even though admission went up to a dollar). Thousands of folks came to the park on excursion boats. Restaurants and

Washington Park entrance with
the Civil War monument.
*Old Lighthouse Museum*

Excursion boats arriving circa 1915.
*Old Lighthouse Museum*

hotels opened downtown to handle the crowds. An attendance
record evidently was set on Saturday, July 25, 1914, when trains
and six steamers arrived with more than ten thousand folks
bound for an afternoon at Washington Park.

Michigan Central Depot, the arrival of a large Excursion Crowd, Michigan City, Ind.

Arrival of a Michigan Central excursion train. *(left) Undated postcard. Mark Stanek*

The WPA Observation Tower. *(below) Undated postcard. Old Lighthouse Museum*

The Zoo opened in 1928 and soon became a destination in its own right. During the Depression, Works Progress Administration workers built sidewalks, stairways, benches, and the Observation Tower. The Michigan City Yacht Club arrived in 1933.

Today, one can't imagine Michigan City without Washington Park. Besides its beach, lighthouse, and marinas, it has restaurants, play areas, the Old Lighthouse Museum, the newly renovated zoo and tower, the band shell, the Senior Center, and the Oasis Splash Park. Annual special events include the Coho Classic, the Super Boat Great Lakes Grand Prix, the Lubeznik Center's Lakefront Art Festival, and the In-Water Boat Show.

Thousands of visitors still come for a day at the park.

*See also: Washington Park Zoo and In-Water Boat Show*

## 1891 Porter Beach and the Great Duneland Scam

Back in 1891, prosperous Chicago was preparing for its first World's Fair. At that time, the newest town in northwest Indiana was East Chicago—a town with a name intended to draw on the popularity of the big city to the northwest. East Chicago even used Chicago's street numbering system. If money could be made in Lake County, why not Porter County?

The lakefront from East Chicago to Michigan City was still rather wild, practically uninhabited, and considered by most civilized folk as undesirable.

So, on July 7, 1891, a plan for the "Lakeshore Addition to the New Stock Yards" was recorded at the Porter County Courthouse. This new subdivision had more than 1,500 tiny (by today's standards) twenty-five-foot lots. The name was deliberately chosen to make folks think that the area was at least near Chicago—the home of the "old" and very flourishing stockyards. Even the street names were part of the hoax. East-west streets were 127th, 128th, 129th, and 130th. North-south streets included Clark, Dearborn, State, Wabash, Michigan, and Indiana. And, of course, there was a Lake Shore Drive, with its seventy-three prestigious lakeshore lots. And the road really did go parallel to the shore. Who would know that it was a full fifty miles south and east of the real Chicago? Of course, there were never any stockyards there.

The lots were advertised in Chicago, and many folks purchased them thinking that they were buying land in, or at least close to, the city. And since these lots were all close to the lake, the prices were higher than for average Chicago lots, and sales were fast-paced.

The new owners were in for a surprise if they tried to visit their lots. There was practically no way to get there. (Dunes Highway wouldn't be built for another thirty years.) In fact, the area was so hilly that one couldn't even build a house on a twenty-five-foot lot. One would have to own three or four lots to build a decent home on the side of a sand dune.

Many of the owners simply abandoned their land, which was then sold at tax sales. However, those who held on to the land, especially those with several lots, made out rather well.

After the Dunes Highway was built in 1923, interest in the area increased. In 1925, the state began purchasing land for Dunes State Park. Recognizing the new value of the lakeshore, the town of Porter annexed the subdivision. The Johnson family paved "Wabash" Avenue for the ease of customers at their restaurant on the beach, but this also made it easier for would-be residents to get to their lots. Many summer cottages have since been built, and in recent years, many fine year-round homes have been constructed. Unfortunately, the lake has claimed the northern portion of the subdivision—what would have been Lake Shore Drive and all seventy-three of its lots are now underwater.

Three of the original street names are still used: Dearborn, Wabash, and State. But 130th Street is now Roskin Road, 129th is Boté Drive, 128th is Duneland Drive, and 127th is Johnson Beach Road.

*See also: Commercial Fishing*

The dunetop 1977 Daisy House designed by Stanley Tigerman. *John and Nancy Lanman*

# 1896 Henry Cowles, Cowles Bog, and Cowles Lodge

Indiana Duneland was Henry Cowles's laboratory. It was to Duneland that he came as a young graduate student in 1896 to do research for his dissertation—resulting in his theory of ecological succession. It was to Duneland that he came as a young professor each year with his students to teach them about botany and ecology. It was to Duneland that as a globally-known and respected researcher he brought international scholars to see this wonder of nature—so close to his University of Chicago.

Henry Cowles arrived at the still-new University of Chicago as a graduate student in 1895. He retired as chair of its botany department in 1934.

In those days, the Michigan Southern Railroad was one of the few ways for Chicagoans to get to the dunes. Thus, Cowles' first experiences with the Indiana Dunes were at the area near the Dune Park station (near today's port) in 1896. He also visited Miller and Chesterton, as there were stations there as well. After the South Shore line was built through the dunes, he could make trips to places east of Dune Park, such as Oak Hill, Mineral Springs, Tremont, and Furnessville. Although Cowles visited many other parts of Duneland, he did some of his most intriguing work at Dune Park. Among other things, Dune Park had migrating dunes advancing on wetlands. In a period of less than a year, he could see significant changes in the landscape. Here he could also see firsthand the development of a sand dune from a small bare mound through stages of stability caused by the growth of marram grass and then of trees such as cottonwoods, juniper and pine. Dr. Cowles conducted his research on dunes and their plant life in several locations, but he returned to the Dune Park area more than the others.

Besides having both stable and moving dunes, Duneland had another great advantage as a place to study ages of landscapes. It is in this part of the greater lake region that the three ancient Lake Michigan shorelines (Glenwood, Calumet, and the high Tolleston) are in close proximity. Thus, in a short time one can walk from the 15,000-year-old Lake Border Moraine past these shorelines, each

Henry Cowles. *Calumet Regional Archives*

Henry Cowles, Sir Arthur Tansley, and others relax during a tour of the dunes. Sir Arthur was the president of the Ecological Society and founder of the *Journal of Ecology. Dunes Learning Center*

Lee Botts, president of the Indiana Dunes Environmental Learning Center, dedicated the center's new central building to Henry Chandler Cowles on Friday, October 9, 1998—nearly a hundred years after Cowles' landmark work was first published. It was only fitting that a learning center lodge be named after Duneland's earliest and foremost educator.
*Dunes Learning Center*

younger than the last, to an active beach where the landscape may be less than a year old.

In observing plant dynamics on dunes, Henry Cowles developed his ideas about "succession," or change in vegetation over time. As he had earlier studied both geology and botany, he was easily able to see relationships between the two disciplines. Cowles' dissertation was published in 1899 under the title "The Ecological Relations of the Vegetation on the Sand Dunes of Lake Michigan." Cowles did not invent the idea of succession, but his study provided an important contribution to this very new idea. He showed how topography, or the shape of the land, influenced succession. He was also able to find patterns of botanical change over time.

Henry Cowles was the first person to identify and draw attention to the strange "quaking" wetland in the dunes west of Mineral Springs Road, where thick vegetation actually floats on water. Year after year, he took his students to see it. In 1913, he made sure that the group of European scholars who came to see the dunes also saw the bog. He made it famous. By the 1920s, people were already referring to this area informally as "Cowles Bog."

Years later, one of the first actions of the Save the Dunes Council was to purchase Cowles Bog at a tax sale. Then in 1964, when the Department of the Interior decided to register unique parcels of land as natural landmarks, the council nominated its special wetland. In 1965, the Secretary of the Interior made the designation official. Cowles and Pinhook Bogs in LaPorte County were the first bogs to be so designated. And with this designation, the Cowles Bog name became official.

## 1896 Octave Chanute and His Flying Machines

Octave Chanute was already well known as a brilliant engineer before he began his experiments in aviation at the Indiana Dunes. The chief engineer for the Erie Railroad, he had designed railroad bridges, flood control dams, and even the Kansas City and Chicago Stockyards. Chanute, Kansas, is named for him.

Chanute's avocation, however, was flying machines. He gathered stories about others who were making and testing flying machines and published a series of twenty-seven articles about aviation in *The Railroad and Engineering Journal.* His book *Progress in Flying Machines* came out in 1894.

Chanute recognized that stability was the primary problem with existing gliders. Being an engineer himself, he decided to design a glider that could be controlled by a pilot with a minimum of effort. He also decided that the soft sands of the Indiana Dunes would be perfect for testing various "machines."

So it was that on June 22, 1896, sixty-two-year-old Octave Chanute, accompanied by his son, Charles, William Avery, and Augustus Herring, took the train from Chicago to the dunes at Miller. Besides provisions and camping gear, they took along two disassembled gliders and a kite.

Octave Chanute. *NPS*

The group walked from the Miller station to an area just northeast of what is now the Lake Street bridge over the Grand Calumet River. They set up camp there and remained for almost two weeks among the high dunes north of the village between the river and the lakeshore. Chanute was basically pleased with the weather, which provided steady enough winds that he could do his experiments. However, he had hoped for privacy. Curious residents of Miller notified the *Chicago Tribune,* which sent out a reporter. On June 24, the *Tribune* ran the story "Men Fly in Midair." This, of course, brought out other reporters and curiosity seekers. Two days later, Chanute told a reporter for Chesterton's *Westchester Tribune,* "We want nothing said of our work or that we are here, because we do not want to be classed with the army of aerial cranks that have been and are exciting the country. We want nothing said in the newspapers and we want no visitors." As might be expected, these very words were published (June 27, 1896), thus attracting even more visitors to come and gawk.

The first design tested was a bat-winged contraption similar to one built and extensively tested earlier by Otto Lilienthal in Germany. Although it was flown many times, and flew up to 116 feet, Chanute described it as awkward and unpredictable. Herring eventually crashed it while landing. Chanute's record of the event ended with, "Glad to be rid of it."

The multi-winged *Katydid.*
*Lake Street Gallery*

They also experimented with the *Katydid,* a glider than Chanute had designed. Although it looked fragile, it handled nicely, but it flew only as far as seventy-six feet. The name "katydid" was used because Chanute and his sons thought the twelve-winged device looked like an insect. (However, a real katydid—the insect—has just four wings. There are lots of katydids in the dunes.)

Armed with his notes and experiences, the team returned to Chicago on July 4 to evaluate their results, make revisions in their designs, and plan another trip out to the dunes.

The team headed back to the dunes on August 20. This time, they were joined by William Paul Butusov, who had worked on gliders in Kentucky, and James Ricketts, a physician with a strong interest in aeronautics. In an attempt to elude reporters, the team went by boat to a place near Dune Park (where US Steel's Midwest Plant is today).

Chanute's three-winged glider didn't work well, but when Herring cut off the bottom wing, the craft did remarkably well. In one attempt, Herring flew 359 feet. This design, which would later be

used by the Wright brothers at Kitty Hawk, North Carolina, was so easy to control that Chanute allowed some of the reporters to try it as well.

Neither Chanute nor Herring invented the biplane; Chanute, however, was the first person to figure out how to use trusses to stabilize and strengthen the wings—similar to the way he stabilized steel bridges.

The experiments were successful. Chanute kept careful records, including the photographs seen here. The results of Chanute's experiments were published in both scientific journals and the popular media. Allowing newspaper reporters to try their luck with the gliders paid great dividends, as their stories thus became more interesting.

Wilbur and Orville Wright asked Chanute for advice concerning their goal of putting a propeller on a bi-winged glider to make a self-propelled flying machine. Chanute made three trips to Kitty Hawk, North Carolina, to advise the Wright brothers. And the rest, as they say, is history.

Chanute campsite at Dune Park.
*(above left) Lake Street Gallery*

Chanute's successful biplane.
*(above right) NPS*

The location of Chanute's experiments.
*K. J. Schoon from an NPS map*

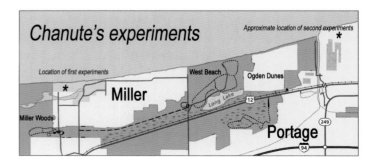

Sheridan Beach on a 1918 postcard.
*Old Lighthouse Museum*

## *1905 LaPorte County Beach Communities*

### Sheridan Beach

Sheridan Beach, to the east of Michigan City's Washington Park, was one of the first residential communities in Indiana established on Indiana's Lake Michigan shoreline. Oscar Wellnitz, a Michigan City baker, built the first house by 1905. The Sheridan Beach Land Company, established in 1907 by William Manny and Isidore Spiro, platted the subdivision and put lots up for sale. Recognizing that some folks would just like to rent a place near the beach for a week or so, Manny and Spiro built "The Pioneer" for vacation rentals. It was a small frame house—the first built on Sheridan Beach Drive.

According to historian Gladys Bull Nicewarner, initial sales were slow because people "could not yet see the sense of building summer homes on what, to them, seemed like a wasteland of worthless sand." People warmed up to the idea as streets and houses were built. Sheridan Beach was finally considered a good investment, and additions to the area were platted. The Sheridan Beach Hotel opened its doors in 1920, by which time Sheridan Beach had become a highly desirable place to live or spend a few days.

## Long Beach

Long Beach is a long and narrow town that parallels its three-mile shoreline. This nature-loving community was the dream of Orrin and Olive Glidden and Orphie Gotto. Part of their plan for developing this part of the shoreline including advertising it in 1914 as having the "Finest Bathing Beach in the World."

In 1921, Long Beach was incorporated as a town, and in 1922, a Spanish-styled clubhouse was built to be the center of not only a new golf course but the whole town. The fact that Long Beach has a golf course is as much related to geography as planning. Much of the Long Beach land was marshland, and the land was simply unsuitable for residential use—but great for greens and fairways.

The roaring twenties were a busy time: a town hall, a school, and four hundred homes were built.

By the year 2000, the number of homes was up to 661, some occupied just in the summer and others year-round residences. The town's population in 2010 was 1,179.

## Duneland Beach

The small community of Duneland Beach got its start in 1920 when Theron Miller purchased sixty acres of land from the Lake Sand Company. One of Miller's stipulations was that no houses were to be built north of Lake Shore Drive—keeping the beach and the lake view open for all.

## Michiana Shores

The town of Michiana Shores is one of Indiana's few land developments that cross state lines. The northern portion is the Michigan town of Michiana while the southern part is Michiana Shores, Indiana. With just a few houses on the lakefront itself,

Four boys ready to dive at the pool at the Long Beach
Country Club (circa 1930). *Old Lighthouse Museum*

much of the land is in the beautiful inland dunes, which are still
wooded.

Much earlier, the eastern part of Michiana Shores was the site
of Corymbo, a logging town started in the 1850s next to a depot of
the Michigan Central Railroad. For a few years, Corymbo was the
center of a small logging operation and had a store, a post office
(probably within the store), and a steam-powered sawmill. By 1876,
according to historian Jasper Packard, the town had twelve log and

frame houses, but only three of them were occupied. The store, post office, and sawmill were already closed. Packard ended his report with, "the prospect for building up a town there is not very flattering." He should see Michigan Shores today!

Orphie Gotto and Clarence Mathias developed the area during the Great Depression. Many of their first houses were "modern" log cabins, which gave a definite rustic flavor to the area. The town of Michiana Shores was incorporated in 1947. It is perhaps best known locally as the home of the Dunes Summer Theater. Its 2010 population was 313.

## 1908 *The South Shore Railroad*

The South Shore got its start in life in 1903 as an East Chicago streetcar line. In 1906–1908, the company constructed a well-engineered interurban electric rail line from Chicago through the dunes to South Bend and built a (pre-NIPSCO) generating station in Michigan City to provide its electricity.

By then called the Chicago, Lake Shore, and South Bend Railway, the line made much of the dunes easily accessible. Residents of Chicago and northwest Indiana could now easily take a morning train to Tremont in the dunes and be back home in time for dinner. Although it has carried both freight and passengers, it is passenger service that has made this railroad, known for years as just the South Shore, the defining railroad of the Calumet Area.

In the 1920s, there were sixteen thousand miles of interurban railroad in the United States and the Lake Shore electric line was one of the fastest. Nevertheless, it soon lost passengers as automobiles became more common. Samuel Insull, president of Chicago Edison Company, purchased the railroad in 1925 at a foreclosure sale and renamed it the Chicago, South Shore & South Bend Railroad. Besides improving service, he created an innovative marketing program that included newsletters and the now well-known poster series. Twenty-five new cars with plush seats, bathrooms, separate smoking compartments, and windows that let in fresh air were purchased in 1926 from the Pullman Company. Ridership increased so fast that the next year Insull ordered twenty more cars.

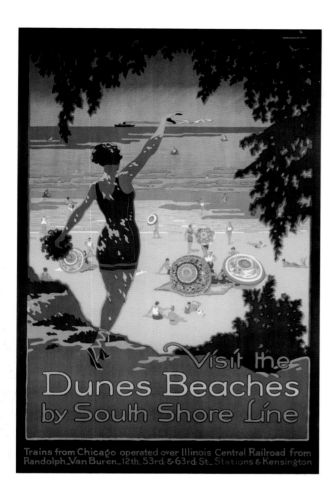

*Visit the Dunes Beaches by South Shore Line.*
1926 lithograph by Otto Brennemann.
*Calumet Regional Archives*

Two of the old cars in Michigan City, 1982.
*(facing top) Calumet Regional Archives*

Boarding the South Shore at Ogden Dunes.
*(facing) Bill Warrick*

Insull decided to take full advantage of the fact that the South Shore was the only line that served the new Indiana Dunes State Park. He started focusing advertising on visits to the dunes, creating dozens of posters advertising the beauty of the dunes area and encouraging Chicagoans to take the train to Duneland. Posters started appearing even before the park was dedicated.

The South Shore was the most successful of all US interurban railroads and is the only one still running. The Great Depression, however, slashed profits, and the line declared bankruptcy in 1933. It survived partly because of its freight service.

In the early years, freight was a minor function of the railroad and was hauled only at night. However, it slowly became the dependably profitable arm of the company. In 1962, the South Shore became the sole provider of coal to the new Bailly Generating Station. The new steel mills and port in Porter County provided new customers. By 1967, the future looked appealing enough that the Chesapeake and Ohio purchased the line. (When profits weren't as high as expected, the C&O sold the line in 1984.)

Passenger service, however, continued to decline and was losing money by the early 1970s. That year, the Interstate Commerce Commission authorized a major reduction in service. By 1976, the C&O was ready to discontinue its passenger service. Early the next year, the Indiana General Assembly created the Northern Indiana Commuter Transportation District (NICTD) and gave it the authority to funnel grant monies to support the passenger service. The NICTD also established a capital improvement program that resulted in the purchase of forty-four new sleek, air-conditioned, stainless-steel cars to replace the then-fifty-seven-year-old, well-used orange cars. By 1983, with the new cars in place, passenger traffic was up to 2.5 million riders a year. Other improvements included several new stations including one at Dune Park (near Chesterton) designed in a style to resemble the smaller original 1929 "Insull Spanish" station at Beverly Shores (still in operation about four miles to the east). New passenger shelters were built at Miller and at Ogden Dunes.

In spite of increased ridership, another financial crisis in 1989 resulted in bankruptcy again. The NICTD then purchased the

railroad's passenger service and ordered more passenger cars. The freight line remained private and profitable.

America's last electric interurban railroad still runs down the middle of streets in Michigan City, and passengers still board the trains streetcar-style (from street level), apparently the only place in the country where this is still done. East of Michigan City, passengers continue to get the real electric interurban rail line experience as the train runs to South Bend past meadows and cornfields on a single-track line.

*See also: Miller, Michigan City, and Beverly Shores*

## 1912 Silent Movies in Duneland

Hernando Cortez and his Spanish conquistadors landing in the new world—actually at the north end of Lake Street in Miller—for the film *The Conquest of Mexico. David Kiehn, Niles Essanay Silent Film Museum*

Back when movies were black and white and talkies hadn't yet been invented, one of the nation's most promising movie production companies was Chicago's Essanay Studio, and one of its filming locations was along the remote lakeshore in northwest Indiana. The dunes made a perfect backdrop for at least a few of Essanay's films. The lake, after all, did quite nicely for ocean scenes, and the beach and dunes could easily become deserts. A bonus was that the dunes were still open and rather empty of homes.

In 1912, Essanay used the dunes at Miller for the *The Conquest of Mexico,* the motion picture spectacular of its day. It was thus at the north end of Lake Street that 160 faux Spaniards led by Hernando Cortez landed on the beach. There they encountered numerous faux Aztecs and their emperor Montezuma, whom they soundly defeated (while dozens of Miller residents looked on from the tops of nearby dunes).

With no hotels in the area, ten Pullman cars sitting on a siding near the Miller Station housed the actors for the week. Many of the "extras" were students from Chicago's Art Institute who enjoyed a Duneland vacation while being paid a dollar a day.

*The Conquest of Mexico,* later renamed *The Fall of Montezuma,* was Essanay's first multi-reel film. (Each reel lasted about fifteen minutes.) According to David Kiehn, historian at the Niles Essanay Silent Film Museum, Essanay publicized it as being filmed in the Southwest, but, perhaps for technical reasons, never released it. One suggestion is that the different cameras used were not aligned with each other, and so perhaps the frame lines were mismatched, and the film couldn't be projected properly.

Two years later, Miller became Mexico again for the filming of the drama *The Plum Tree.* America's first "matinee idol," Francis X. Bushman, described as the handsomest man in America, starred in that film.

### *Lost in the Desert*

Powell Moore related the story of the Dunes Park filming of *Lost in the Desert.* This elaborate 1919 film involved actors portraying British soldiers, Bedouin warriors, and Arab women along with, of course, horses and camels. In the last scene, the leading man, playing the part of a British officer with torn clothing, unkempt hair and beard, and a heavy club, escapes from the Bedouin bandits and wanders aimlessly around the desert until rescued. When the filming was completed, the actor fell asleep in the shade of a tree. The company, however, packed up its equipment and returned to Miller.

According to Moore, the actor wasn't missed until the cast and crew got back to Miller, when it was too late and dark for a search party to return to the dunes.

When the actor awoke, he wandered about but couldn't find anyone or any sign of civilization. Eventually he fell asleep in the dunes, alone except for the mosquitoes. The next morning, a hunter from the nearby town of Crisman saw the "ragged, unkempt, half-naked man with long hair and a beard stumbling through the sand, carrying a club." The hunter hurried back to town and reported what he saw, and a sheriff's posse eventually tracked down and rescued the lost man before dark. He was indeed, one could say, lost in the desert.

## 1915 Diana of the Dunes

Of all the people who have lived in the dunes, the best known still today and perhaps the least understood is Alice Mabel Gray, far better known as Diana of the Dunes.

Alice arrived in the dunes in 1915 before the Dunes Highway was built and before the Porter County lakeside residential communities were established. The dunes she came to know so well were still wild, inaccessible, and unknown to most folk. In the ten years she lived there, she became a local legend largely because several newspaper reporters felt no need to stick to the truth. Fiction apparently sold more newspapers than facts.

Reporters claimed that she was a beautiful young woman who bathed naked in the lake and then danced around like a nymph to dry off. From early on, she was incorrectly described as the daughter of a well-to-do Chicago doctor. She was said to be like a goddess—the goddess of the woodlands, of wild animals, of the hunt, and of the moon. She was the Roman goddess Diana, "Diana of the Dunes." Long after her death, her ghost is said to still inhabit the dunes. In fact, nearly a hundred years after her arrival, Wikipedia claims that Diana of the Dunes is one of the best-known ghost legends of Indiana. The ghost seems to always be either wearing a long, flowing gown or bathing sans attire in the waters of the lake. There's a section about Diana and her ghost in *Weird Indiana* by Mark Marimen, James Willis, and Troy Taylor.

Most Northwest Indiana Hoosiers today couldn't tell you who Alice Gray was, but they very well might have heard of Diana of the Dunes.

Thanks to ten years of extensive research by Janet Zenke Edwards, assisted by many folks including Jane Walsh Brown and Eva Hopkins at the Westchester Public Library, we now know more about Alice Gray than folks have at any time since her death in 1925.

Alice was the daughter of Ambrose and Sally Gray and grew up on the South Side of Chicago in a working-class family. Alice did well in school. She earned an academic excellence award in high school and after graduating in 1897 started taking classes at the nearby University of Chicago. It took her seven years, but the persistent Alice worked as a stenographer while enrolled and in 1903 graduated with a bachelor of arts. The mathematics department gave her its highest academic honor.

After graduation, Alice moved to Washington, DC, and for three years worked for the US Naval Observatory. She then went to Germany and enrolled at the University of Gottingen, where it is believed that she studied higher mathematics.

One account notes that while there, Alice was introduced to Wandervogel, a German youth organization. Wandervogel was similar in some ways to American Scouting, but it emphasized more of a "back-to-nature" philosophy. Its origins were a reaction to industrialization, automation, materialism, and child labor. The Wandervogel website notes that it has been described as the first hippie movement. It certainly is true that Alice developed many Wandervogel philosophies.

Then it was back to the University of Chicago, where she took several additional math courses followed by a couple in philosophy. Her last class was in 1913.

## Off to the Dunes

We know little of the next two years of her life except that in the fall of 1915, she took the South Shore to the Wilson Stop and got off to live alone in the dunes.

Why she left Chicago is still not fully known. She refuted writers who said that her departure from Chicago was because of a love affair gone bad. What is known is that she was terribly depressed on the day of her arrival at the dunes and had considered "ending it all." However once in Duneland, her spirits improved.

Alice soon wrote in her diary, "How exquisite the bare hills stand out . . . especially in the subdued light at sunset."

At first she wondered what she would do when she returned to Chicago. However, after a few days in the dunes, she decided that she'd never go back. She then spent the winter of 1915–16 alone, learning to survive among the hills and woods south of the lakeshore and beginning to realize that she was indeed living her dream.

Alice Gray, aka Diana of the Dunes
*Indianapolis Star,* February 12, 1925

Driftwood. *Westchester Township History Museum*

Her first four nights were spent in the open, but then she discovered an abandoned shack, perhaps built by George Blagge, an earlier Duneland recluse. It was roughly made and had no windows, but it was not wanted by anyone else, and so it became her home—she called it "Driftwood." She also found a teepee sheltered by high dunes in an area that would later become Dune Acres. The teepee was used by Chicago naturalists William and Flora Richardson on their frequent visits to the dunes. Apparently, when Alice was near the teepee late in the day if the Richardsons weren't around, she made use of its shelter.

Alice learned to hunt and to gather berries. She was not a hermit; rather, she just wanted to live alone on her own terms. She would walk to downtown Porter or to her sister's home in Michigan City, and she was well known to residents along the south edge of the dunes. Agnes Larson, who had a home on Howe Road, would invite her in for coffee, conversation, and fresh Swedish limpa (rye) bread and would sell her food or lend her books. Alice had a card for the public library in Miller and was known to borrow "armloads" of books.

Of course, Alice bathed naked in the lake—but only when it was warm enough to do so. The only way to keep her clothes dry was to take them off before going into the water.

## Discovery and Unwanted Fame

Alice Gray's solitude ended after just nine months.

Apparently, a fisherman's wife, perhaps unhappy with her husband's reports of a naked woman on the beach, notified the *Chicago Tribune.* Local newspapers picked up the story and sent reporters to find her. Not knowing (or initially caring) who she was, the articles were designed to entice, not to inform.

The *Lake County Times* ran a story on July 22, 1916, with the headline "Mystic Nymph in Wild Dunes" and speculated that twice every day "the nymph of the dunes, whose name is not known, takes her plunge like a goddess of the wave." One reporter nicknamed her "Diana of the Dunes," and the name stuck.

Alice loved the dunes. She was quoted in the *Chicago Herald* and *Examiner* as saying, "how wonderful, how unspeakably healing and sanctifying it has been living in all this beauty and this keenly vital air and in the blessed solitude."

The only known photo of Alice Gray smiling. © *Chicago Tribune Company*

Alice supported the efforts to create a Sand Dunes National Park even though that action would take away her solitude. In April of 1917, she spoke in favor of the park at a lecture at Chicago's Art Institute.

> Besides its nearness to Chicago and its beauty, its spiritual power, there is between the Dune Country and the city a more than sentimental bond—a family tie. To see the Dunes destroyed would be for Chicago the sacrilegious sin which is not forgiven."
>
> —ALICE GRAY, "Chicago's Kinland," an essay read in Chicago, April 6, 1917

Alice participated in the planning of the Dunes Pageant in 1917. Sometime around early 1918, Alice met Paul Wilson. They became inseparable. Where she was small in stature, he was big (at 6'2" and 225 pounds). While her conversation reflected her education, his was often brash and crude. Although she invited almost no one into her cabin, she invited Paul to move in. The two of them were devoted to each other. Janet Edwards noted that reporters often referred to him as "Alice's caveman." He called her Diana, not Alice.

For some reason, perhaps because too many people knew where to find them, Paul and Alice left Driftwood and either found or built a new cabin on undeveloped land owned by Francis Ogden. (Today's Diana Road in Ogden Dunes is named for Alice.) They named it Wren's Nest.

By this time, the dunes were becoming a destination, not just for the Prairie Club and occasional hikers but for youth groups as well. A Boy Scout camp was soon established not far from the Wren's Nest. As can be expected, the Scouts were forbidden to visit the cabin, in spite of the fact that Paul made a couple of rowboats for their use. Reporters apparently tired of their Duneland adventures, and so Alice and Paul were finally left alone.

Left alone, that is, until 1922. That June, Alice and Paul were suspected of killing a man whose body was found elsewhere in the dunes. In spite of the fact that the county sheriff told Alice that she was not under suspicion, Chicago and local newspapers again started printing sensational accounts about them with little regard to evidence. When Paul and Alice had all of the hounding they could take, they went to confront Eugene Frank, their main accuser. The ensuing altercation resulted in Paul's being shot and Alice's skull being fractured. She was hospitalized for several weeks. Frank was charged with shooting with intent to kill. Alice later filed a libel suit against the *Chicago American*.

The year 1923 was eventful for Duneland. That spring, Dunes State Park was authorized by the Indiana General Assembly. The much-awaited Dunes Highway (now Route 12) opened in November and soon became the state's busiest highway. And even before the highway was completed, Ogden Dunes and Dune Acres were platted. Finally, plans were being made for the construction of Burns Ditch, which in 1926 cut through the dunes and beach and thus made it nearly impossible for folks like Alice to walk across the area.

Alice's dunes were attracting hundreds, soon thousands, of visitors. So, reluctantly, she and Paul left for Texas. But things didn't work out, and six months later they returned to Wren's Nest.

Alice died on February 9, 1925. The cause of death was kidney failure. But even in death, Alice was "Diana." Newspapers across the country ran the story of her death. Most surprising was the headline of the *Helena* (Montana) *Independent,* which stated, "Diana of Dunes is Dead, Dancing in Moonlight on Sands of Shore at End."

Alice was buried in Gary's Oak Hill Cemetery. With Paul's approval, the Wren's Nest was demolished.

## 1915 *The Prairie Club and the* NDPA

The Prairie Club was the first group to propose that a significant section of the dunes along the Lake Michigan shoreline be set aside, maintained in its natural state, and remain open to the public for its benefit and enjoyment.

The Prairie Club was a Chicago organization started in 1911 by outdoor enthusiasts that regularly scheduled hikes out to the dunes. Although Prairie Club outings were held in many locations, the Indiana Dunes became a favorite locale. The Club purchased forty-nine acres of land in the dunes (in what is now Dunes State Park), including a half-mile of shoreline. Its beach house east of Mount Tom had a broad veranda, living room, kitchen, and sleeping quarters that could accommodate sixty people. It was in this house that the club had gatherings and planned for the preservation of the area that they had come to so appreciate.

The Prairie Club celebrated the Dunes and held several masques (plays) in nearby blow-outs, which were natural amphitheaters. On Memorial Day, 1915, it staged a masque called *The Awakening* in front of 1,200 spectators. The plot was simple but the production fanciful, perhaps extravagant:

A young man awakens to the beauties of Duneland as summer approaches and Helios [the sun] and Sylvan [the forest] awaken. The young man then joins the walking club and returns frequently to the Dunes.

Members could see how Lake Michigan's shoreline was quickly being changed from a rather inaccessible but starkly beautiful wilderness to a line of heavy industry that was closing the lakefront to public use. Not only had the lakefront become valuable but so had

Boarding the South Shore for the return trip to Chicago after a hike. *Arthur Anderson, Calumet Regional Archives*

Two dancers in *The Awakening*, May 31, 1915.
*Arthur Anderson, Calumet Regional Archives*

the sand. The Hoosier Slide, once the tallest sand dune on the Lake Michigan shoreline, was nearly gone. The club established a conservation committee composed of well-known landscape architect Jens Jensen, botanist Henry Cowles, Thomas Allinson, and Stephen Mather, who would later become the first director of the National Park Service.

In 1916, Congress created the National Park Service and Indiana created its state park system. While the national parks debate was occurring in Washington, concerned citizens in the Chicago/Calumet region decided to work toward forming the first national park east of the Mississippi River.

In July of that year, fearing that Mt. Tom might soon be leveled, Prairie Club members voted to form the National Dunes Park Association (NDPA). This new organization would actively promote the establishment of a national park along the shoreline. Elected officers were Armanis F. Knotts, Thomas H. Cannon, and Bess Sheehan. On the board of directors were Jens Jensen, Henry Cowles, John O. Bowers, and George Pinneo.

At first, prospects looked very good. After Congress established the National Park Service in August, Prairie Club member Steven Mather was named its first director. Within two weeks, Mather had met with Indiana Senator Thomas Taggart, who then submitted a resolution to the Senate calling on the Secretary of the Interior to explore a dune park's feasibility. The Senate approved the resolution, and in October, Mather, representing the Secretary, made a one-week trip from Washington to Chicago to hold a public hearing and see the Dunes.

The courtroom in the Chicago Federal Building where the hearing was held was neatly decorated with Earl Reed's sketches of the dunes, and an exhibit featuring prickly pear cactus was at the front. The hearing was attended by four hundred people. Forty-two of them, including Dr. Cowles, artist Earl Reed, and a representative of the Potawatomi tribe spoke in favor of the park. No one spoke against it. Dr. Cowles noted that since his work on plant succession there, the Dunes had come to be known throughout the world for their ecological importance, and that scientists had come from all over to study there.

Grace Albright (second from the right), then recently married to Horace Albright, the first assistant director of the National Park Service, and others hike through the dunes during a 1916 tour. *NPS*

Stephen Mather (far left) and Richard Lieber lead a hike through the Indiana Dunes, October 1916, as part of the Interior Department hearings. *NPS*

Besides the formal hearing in Chicago, Stephen Mather's assignment included touring the dunes. And so a group composed of Mather, Horace Albright (the first assistant director of the National Park Service), his new wife Grace Albright, Richard Lieber (chairman of the Indiana state park committee), NDPA members, and a photographer made the trip to the dunes.

In his report, Mather emphasized that a national park was justified because of the characteristics of the dunes, including their plant and animal life. But in addition, the proximity of the dunes to the homes of five million people meant that it could be easily accessed by more people than any other park in the nation. As Congress hadn't allocated any funds for the project, Stephen Mather published the report at his own expense and submitted it to Secretary Lane in December of 1916.

Support for the park was by no means universal. Opposition came from Porter County political and business leaders, who felt that such a large park would undermine the tax base and not allow the county to benefit from the type of industry that was providing so many jobs and tax dollars to Lake County.

Hope, however, turned to apprehension in just a few months. Even before Mather's report was completed, Senator Taggart, the congressional champion of the dunes, was defeated in the November election. In the spring of 1917, Mather suffered a nervous breakdown and ceased his promotion of the park, and then, on April 6, the United States entered World War I. National priorities changed overnight.

## The Dunes Under Four Flags

A nation at war cannot forget homeland issues, and the National Dunes Park Association wanted to make sure that the local population remembered that the dunes still needed protection. So the NDPA decided to expand the Prairie Club's annual spring festival and stage a historical pageant right in the middle of the dunes themselves. Called *The Dunes Under Four Flags*, the extravaganza would combine patriotism, history, poetry, music, and dance.

Pageants were quite popular in these days before folks had either radio or television in their homes. There was even an American Pageant Association. So in February of 1917, when local organizers formed the Dunes Pageant Association, they commissioned its president, Thomas Wood Stevens, a successful pageant writer, to compose a grand one for the Dunes.

The date was set for Memorial Day (a Wednesday—Memorial Day was then always May 30). It was decided to hold the pageant in the "Big Blowout" at Waverly Beach (today, west of the pavilion). That location would allow for a large crowd to see the program. For the next several months:

- Organizers arranged for speakers, choirs, and bands,
- Choreographers designed the dances and recruited the dancers to portray wood nymphs, spirits, and elves,
- Directors were appointed and found actors to play the parts of American Indians, Marquette, fur trappers, British and Spanish soldiers, pioneers, and even Daniel Webster,
- Volunteers were lined up to sew costumes, and
- Everybody started rehearsals.

Newspapers spread the word. Thanks largely to the efforts of Bess Sheehan, local women's clubs helped organize nation-wide publicity including the making and showing of newsreels that were shown in movie palaces.

On Memorial Day, the huge cast and about thirty thousand people arrived for the program. It was scheduled to begin at 2:30, but many folks arrived much earlier so that they could spend the full holiday at the dunes. However, the skies were threatening, and many feared that it would rain.

Historian George Brennan, who had helped with the history sections of the pageant script, was there, and he described the event this way:

> The pageant was started with Donald Robertson, the Pageant Master. In a rich solemn voice that swelled over that vast audience, he depicted the love of the Indians for the Dune country, and their sorrow at leaving it. At one time he called on Great Manitou to show his love for the Indians and their beloved home, the beautiful Dunes, and then stood with upraised arms, awaiting an answer. . . . While still in his pose of supplication, the heavens opened with a fierce electric display all over the lake and the Dunes, followed by continuous, deafening crashes of thunder, reverberating through the hills and valleys, which continued for some time.
> It was thrilling; yea, awe-inspiring!

Part of the audience of 25,000 persons who saw the pageant on June 3. *A. E. Ormes from the Prairie Club Archives at the Westchester Township History Museum*

Within a few minutes, the rains started pouring down, and the pageant was momentarily suspended. After that downpour, an attempt was made to restart the program, but the rains returned. The event was canceled, and the audience was encouraged to return for the already-scheduled Sunday performance on June 3.

Sunday was a beautiful day, and some twenty-five thousand people found their way back to Waverly Beach. The sun was bright, and the sight of musicians and seven hundred actors preparing for the event made the audience realize that it was in for a treat. The pageant this time went off without a hitch. At its close, there was a grand review of all seven hundred actors, who led the crowd in the singing of patriotic songs while a flag was raised on Mount Tom. It was a great day.

The cast included nine girls in the mosquito dance, sixteen girls as nymphs, sixteen men as satyrs, a hundred Indians, twenty Frenchmen with LaSalle, ninety-five in the Revolutionary War scene, twenty fur traders, forty in the Spanish march, and thirty pioneers.

To keep the spirit of the event alive after it was over, the organizers sent copies of the pageant program to each member of Congress. In spite of the apparent success of the pageant, Congress and the American people were more concerned with the war than national parks. By 1919, apprehension changed to despair. During

Dance of the waves. *(facing top)*
Interpretive dancers. *(facing left)*
The bird dance. *(facing right)*
*All photos on facing page by James Pondelicek, from the Prairie Club Archives at the Westchester Township History Museum*

*Sunday's program*

the war, there was no chance that federal monies would be available for a park, yet sand mining of the dunes continued unabated while opposition to the park grew stronger.

After the war ended on November 11, 1918, the movement floundered. On May 15, 1919, the NDPA voted to drop its efforts to establish a national park and instead attempt to convince the Hoosier General Assembly to create a state park.

## 1922 *The Dunes Highway*

By the 1920s, folks were buying cars, and travel by automobile was becoming common—yet paved rural roads were still a rare treat.

What is now Route 12 between Gary and Michigan City was proposed in 1918 by the Dunes Highway Association, a group of representatives of northwest Indiana lakeside cities. Construction began in March, 1922. The section from Michigan City to Baileytown followed the ancient Calumet Shoreline/Chicago–Detroit stage road and was easier to build than the western section, which crossed the Great Marsh. With great fanfare, the highway opened in November, 1923. The only concrete highway in northern Porter County, it was immediately used by tourists, commuters, and cross-continental travelers. As the most direct route between Detroit and Chicago (as the Chicago–Detroit stagecoach route had been ninety years earlier), it soon became the busiest highway in Indiana.

The highway spurred development. It is no accident that so many communities (as well as Dunes State Park) were all established in the 1920s.

The new Dunes Highway, 1922.
*Calumet Regional Archives*

When Route 20 was built several years later, it was referred to by many as the "Dunes Relief Highway." Interstate 94 relieved it even more, so much so that driving the Dunes Highway today (except around the mills' shift change) can be a quiet and serene experience.

# 1923 *Dune Acres and Ogden Dunes*

Dune Acres and Ogden Dunes are built on the sand dunes immediately south of the present shoreline. Had Indiana's northern boundary not been moved north by ten miles when Indiana became a state in 1816, most of Ogden Dunes and all of Dune Acres would today still be in Michigan.

The two communities are incorporated towns, each extending from the lakeshore to about the South Shore Railroad and Route 12. The building of the railroad in 1906–1908 increased awareness and interest in this lakeshore area, but it was the building of the Dunes Highway (Route 12) that really made it possible for these two communities to get started.

## Dune Acres

Two of the first people living in the Dune Acres area, arriving long before the town was even planned, were Chicagoans William and Flora Richardson. They built a small hut (replaced later by a modern home) at what later became the western part of the town, and they would come out to the dunes on weekends. Intensely fond of the dunes and their wildlife, they slowly built up a large collection of books about nature. William, an amateur photographer, took more than eight thousand photographs of plants and animals in the Duneland area. When the Richardsons died, they left their collection to the Richardson Wildlife Sanctuary, a non-profit organization dedicated to education, research, and the preservation of the natural history and ecology of the southern Lake Michigan region. For many years, the organization maintained a lending library and distributed environmental education materials from the Richardson home.

In 1922, before the Dunes Highway was officially open, Gary Schools Superintendent William A. Wirt procured a ninety-nine-year lease of about 580 acres from Henry Leman. According to historian Powell Moore, this land contained some of the highest dunes along the south shore of the lake. Dune Acres was platted in 1923 just west of the proposed Indiana Dunes State Park and about

One of the many log homes built in Dune Acres.
*Arthur Anderson, Calumet Regional Archives*

two miles north of the old Chellberg Farm. Wirt, Arthur Melton, and other Gary residents envisioned Dune Acres as an upscale lakeside residential area away from the industrial shores in Lake County. Following an August 1923 election with nine votes in favor and none against, Dune Acres was incorporated as a town.

Amenities such as the clubhouse, a guest house, and golf course were soon developed and helped give the new town its character.

The clubhouse still serves the community. In the south part of the town is Cowles Bog, now part of the Indiana Dunes National Lakeshore.

In 1924, William Wirt's nephew, Alden Studebaker, was hired as superintendent of construction. Besides creating the water system, maintaining the roads, completing the clubhouse, and building about thirty of the houses, he arranged for OttoMina Chellberg to cater several of the dinners at the new clubhouse. Soon he and OttoMina were married. Their son Henry was the first Dunes Acres child. The early roads, by the way, were unpaved—just consisting of crushed stone and clay. According to Naomi Studebaker, there were frequent washouts.

In spite of the Depression, lot sales and home building continued during the 1930s. It was during this time that several of the log homes were built, all constructed using logs brought in by train from Oregon. Dune Acres at that time was primarily a summer resort community. Until 1946, mail was only delivered from June 1 to September 15. The place was nearly empty in the winter. It was in the decades following World War II that many families started living in town year-round.

Through the years, Dune Acres has managed to maintain its low-density housing set in the forested Duneland environment. Residents take pride in living in an area where the natural hilly landscape has been so carefully preserved. Its population in 2010 was 182.

Dune Acres Club House: Serving the community since 1926. To the right is the old guest house.
*Arthur Anderson, Calumet Regional Archives*

## Ogden Dunes

Before the Dunes Highway was built, what is now Ogden Dunes was a desolate tract of dunes. The only known residents were Alice Gray (Diana of the Dunes) and her husband, Paul Wilson, who lived in a shack near Polliwog Pond in the northwest section of the current town. Local Boy and Girl Scout troops used the area for

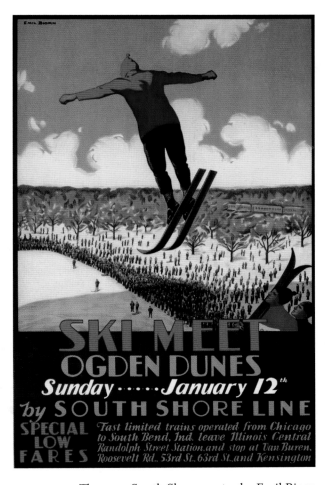

The 1929 South Shore poster by Emil Biorn encouraging Chicagoans to take the train to see the January 12 ski meet. *Calumet Regional Archives*

summer camping expeditions. In 1919, the Inland Steel Company supplied lumber and building materials for a permanent lakeshore camping headquarters named "Camp Win-Sum" because it could be used in both winter and summer. It had a long enclosed porch that faced the lake.

In 1923, Samuel Reck purchased 513 acres of Duneland in order to develop a residential community in the dunes. The streets and lots were then platted by Colin Mackenzie, and the area was named for Francis Ogden, who earlier had owned much of the land between the county line and what is now Burns Ditch. From the beginning, Ogden Dunes was to be a residential community with no commercial establishments. Like Dune Acres, however, Ogden Dunes was to have had a harbor for small pleasure craft, a hotel, and a golf course complete with clubhouse.

The Ogden Dunes Realty Company was formed to sell lots, but sales were slow—largely because access was so difficult. In 1925, all twenty-four residents unanimously voted to incorporate the area as a town. According to historian Powell Moore, this was done partially so that the town could build an entrance road across the New York Central tracks.

It is hard today to imagine how isolated the community was in the early days. The only utility was electricity. There were no paved roads, no mail delivery, and no gas lines or city water.

In 1927, the Grand Beach (later Ogden Dunes) Ski Club bought land on one of the high dunes on the south side of town and built a world-class ski jump. The main tower at the top end of the slide was as high as a twenty-two-story building. Said to be highest man-made slide in the country, it was featured in a well-known South Shore advertising poster. Partly because of the South Shore's advertising, the ski jump attracted large crowds, but it was closed about six years later, a victim of the Great Depression.

Residential growth in the town was slow, particularly of year-round residents (generally, the only ones who were counted in the census and who could vote). By 1930, Ogden Dunes had just fifty permanent residents. The population in 2010 was 1,110.

The town really blossomed after World War II. The first unit of the firehouse was built, with volunteer labor, in 1949. Families in town were all asked to contribute $50 to the cause. Those monies were augmented by proceeds from the annual Fireman's Ball.

As the town grew, social and civic organizations were established. The first was the Women's Club in 1938. Boy Scout Troop 68 was founded in 1944, the fire department in 1948, the Ogden Dunes Community Church in 1953, the Home Association in 1957, the Lions Club in 1958, and the Garden Club in 1974. However, the most influential group founded in town was the Save the Dunes Council, founded in 1952 in the home of Dorothy Buell, its first president.

## 1923 *Inland Towns*

### Tremont

Tremont, located immediately south of the state park, is the site of the Green Tavern, a stagecoach inn built in the 1830s. The name "Tremont" refers to the three highest dunes in the area, Mt. Tom, Mt. Holden, and Mt. Jackson. The South Shore Railroad in 1908 and the Dunes Highway in 1923 made transportation to Tremont convenient, and many families decided to live "back of the dunes." After Indiana Dunes State Park was established in 1926, the South Shore's Tremont Station became an important stop on that line. Tremont, synonymous with the dunes, is included within the boundaries of the National Lakeshore.

Many years ago . . .

Within the tract now known as Ogden Dunes, my old friend, Tom Stearns . . . owned a tract of eighty acres. One day Tom came over to my place to buy two pigs at $2 apiece, he said he did not have the money to pay for them, but would give me the eighty acres for them. I told him to take the pigs home with him and pay me for them when he could get the money. This land sold a few years ago for about $800 per acre. Now I cannot raise enough pigs in ten years to purchase even a fifty-foot lot in those subdivisions in the Knobs.

It takes a pretty good prophet to foretell, long in advance, the events and conditions of the Calumet Region.

—DARUS BLAKE, 1929

The Tremont Hotel was a private home that was enlarged and converted into a hotel (or bed and breakfast) after the state park was opened and catered to out-of-town visitors. *Westchester Township History Museum*

Roeske's Mill, early twentieth century.
*Ed Hedstrom Collection*

## Pines

Pines is situated on the narrow strip of Calumet Shoreline dunes south of and parallel to Route 12. The town, located in Pine Township in the northeast corner of Porter County, was planned by William Schleman soon after the highway was built in 1922–23. It and the township were named after the great pine trees that once covered much of the area. Pines was incorporated as a town in 1952. It is home to Duneland's oldest still-operating motels and Indiana's shortest highway—Indiana Route 520, between Routes 12 and 20. Its population in 2010 was 217.

## Trail Creek

Back in 1832, John Walker constructed a dam across Trail Creek and built the area's first sawmill. Walker was kept busy providing lumber for all the new residents coming to the new Michigan City. In later years, the mill was converted to a flour mill, which in 1880 was purchased by brothers Christopher and August Roeske. The Roeskes expanded their business ventures by establishing the Roeske Brick Yards, getting their raw material, glacial clay, from where the Michigan City Fish and Game Club was later located.

The community that grew up around the mills and brick yards came to be known informally as Roeskeville, and its residents always felt a bit separate from the larger city to the west. When in 1923 it was feared that Roeskeville might be annexed by Michigan City, the residents decided to incorporate as an independent town. The incorporation was approved by LaPorte County in 1924, and the town of Trail Creek became an entity. Its population in 2010 was 2,052.

## Pottawattamie Park

Pottawattamie Park, a small independent town completely surrounded by Michigan City, is the home of the International Friendship Gardens and the Pottawattamie Country Club. As Michigan City grew to the east, the residents of this neighborhood decided that they wished to maintain their independence and so, following Trail Creek's lead, incorporated as a town in 1936. Because it's the site of what George Brennan in 1923 called a Potawatomi "council ground," it was decided to adopt the name Pottawattamie Park. Its population in 2010 was 235.

# 1926 Burns Ditch

The Little Calumet River, like many of the lowland areas between the various former Lake Michigan shorelines, has long been prone to flooding. As urban development increased and farming became more intensive, these floods came to cause much damage. Burns Ditch was designed to help solve flooding problems by connecting the Little Calumet River in Porter County directly to the lake. To create it, seven new railroad bridges had to be constructed and more than 2.5 million cubic yards of sand removed. Completed in 1926, it was named after Randall W. Burns, a local farmer and real estate developer who owned 1,200 acres of previously "worthless" wetlands and strongly promoted its construction. The ditch cut through a mile of sand dunes. At the same time, several miles of the riverbed were straightened in an attempt to improve water flow. This project was done at a time when wetlands were considered not only wasteful but dangerous. Draining them was referred to as "reclaiming" land.

Burns Waterway when new in 1926. Today, United States Steel's Midwest Plant is east of the waterway (to the left), and the Portage Lakefront and Riverwalk is to the west (right). *NPS*

The completion of the ditch was celebrated by folks who were hampered by the river's periodic flooding. Their land could then be farmed or subdivided as residential neighborhoods.

Since the construction of the ditch, river water from LaPorte and eastern Porter Counties no longer flows westward into Lake County but instead north through Burns Ditch into Lake Michigan. Also, river water in western Porter County and eastern Lake County now flows east and then north into the lake. Thus, the Little Calumet River now has the distinction of flowing in two directions. The far western part of the river (from about the Munster/Highland border) still flows westward into Illinois.

One perhaps unexpected development along Burns Waterway, as it is now named, is the appearance of the many marinas that now provide safe harbor for pleasure boats.

## 1926 *Indiana Dunes State Park*

Indiana Dunes State Park is one of Indiana's most popular state parks. Besides the beach, it has a landscape that is beautiful, inspiring, and historic. Dunes State Park has for years been the second-most-visited park in the Indiana state park system.

The three tallest dunes in the park are

- Mt. Tom, at 192 feet, probably named for Tom Brady, who was captured by British soldiers at the Battle of Petite Fort in 1780,
- Mt. Holden, at 184 feet, named for Edward J. Holden, president of the Prairie Club of Chicago, for his and the club's efforts to establish the park, and
- Mt. Jackson, at 176 feet, named for Indiana Governor Edward L. Jackson in gratitude for his support of the park when that support was so vital.

The eastern two-thirds of the park is the Dunes Nature Preserve. It contains the three dunes listed above, blowouts, and extensive wetlands and woodlands. Much of the preserve is accessible by established trails that range in length from ¾ to 5½ miles and in difficulty from easy to rugged. Hikers on trail 8, the most strenuous, climb all three of the highest dunes.

Indiana Dunes State Park was one of the first tangible results of the "Save the Dunes" efforts of the early twentieth century. The park was proposed by Richard Lieber, the first director of the Indiana Department of Conservation and the "father" of the Indiana State Park system, who declared in 1922 that it was "the privilege and duty of Indiana, with private assistance, to preserve this heritage and God-given spot." He proposed purchasing about two thousand acres along three miles of Lake Michigan's shoreline. To finance it, he suggested a one-cent tax increase on each $500 of personal property over seven years.

If Lieber was the father of the state park system, then surely Bess Sheehan can be called the mother of Indiana Dunes State Park. Mrs. Sheehan had been the secretary of the earlier National Dunes Park Association and was the chair of the Dunes Park Committee of the Indiana Federation of [Women's] Clubs, which represented six hundred Indiana chapters. This organization was already a powerful lobbying group just two years after women in the United States were granted the right to vote. Sheehan personally lobbied state legislators in 1923 and even gave a stereopticon lecture before a special joint evening session of the legislature to which legislators' wives had been invited. Sheehan's presentation eloquently presented both the beauty of the area and the arguments for its preservation. Her efforts paid off: the assembly approved the park.

However, state funds couldn't be used to purchase land until 1930, when the tax monies would be collected. In the meantime, with the Dunes Highway finished, land prices were rising so rapidly that it was becoming very likely that the funds collected by the tax wouldn't cover the cost of purchase and the park would never be created. Lieber and Sheehan realized that time was running out and so began an ambitious but initially disappointing fund-raising campaign. The turning point came when Indiana governor Jackson accepted Lieber's invitation to visit the Dunes. After doing so, he authorized the spending of state funds already collected in order to purchase land.

Waverly Beach (where the Pavilion is today) was already a popular spot in 1926. The Prairie Club and many individual families had purchased small plots of land and had built summer houses there.

Bess Sheehan, president of the Indiana Federation of [Women's] Clubs.
*Cannon, Loring and Robb, 1927*

Atop Mount Tom, attorney and historian John O. Bowers hands the deed for 110 acres including Mount Tom to Governor Jackson (far left). *Indiana Dunes State Park*

The Johnson family had a successful fishing business there with a popular restaurant.

Hoping to set a precedent, Gary historian John O. Bowers sold his land (containing Mt. Tom) at half its market value. Julius Rosenwald, president of Sears and Roebuck, gave $50,000, US Steel donated $250,000, and the South Shore Railroad donated land for the entranceway as well as $25,000 toward the cost of building a

bathhouse (pavilion) and resort hotel. Samuel Insull, owner of the railroad, personally donated funds so that electric lines would be installed underground. The railroad then often featured the scenery and activities at the park in its advertising posters. Chicagoans were, of course, urged to take the train to see the dunes.

## The Park Opens

On July 1, 1926, four years ahead of the original schedule, Indiana Dunes State Park opened to the public with three miles of beach and about 3 ½ square miles (2,182 acres) of land. In the first three months, nearly 63,000 people came to visit.

The Department of Conservation immediately began developing the parkland.

- The parking lot at Waverly Beach was expanded.
- 1,300 feet of Dunes Creek (formerly called Fort Creek) was diverted into an underground culvert so that the parking lot could be enlarged again.
- Trails were created and a fire tower built atop Mt. Jackson.
- The limestone pavilion was built and opened in 1929. This structure, right on the beach, contained a restaurant and general store on the ground level and changing and shower

223

The Dunes Arcade Hotel and the Pavilion, 1930s.
*Indiana Dunes State Park*

The Pavilion and lot. Note that Dunes Creek is buried under the parking lot and emerges from a culvert near the shore (on the left). The Devil's Slide dune is on the far left. *(facing top)*

A double line of cars at the entrance to Dunes State Park, 1955. *(facing bottom)*
*Both photos by Arthur Anderson, Calumet Regional Archives*

facilities on the second floor. The roof was originally open to the public and contained a children's playground.

· The Dunes Arcade Hotel opened for business in August of 1931 with forty-four very small guest rooms. Immediately west of the Pavilion, it was designed by Long Beach architect John Lloyd Wright with an Oriental Art-Deco/Expressionist design. The hotel operated on the "American Plan," meaning that three meals a day (served in the Pavilion) were included in the stated price. Washrooms were down the hall from the guest rooms. The hotel proved to be unworkable and was demolished in 1972.

· The road from the Dunes Highway (US 12) into the park was improved (in 1931) on the strip of land donated by the South Shore Railroad.

In 1933, the Depression-era Civilian Conservation Corps established a camp in the park. For the next nine years, Corps members helped maintain the park, cleared ground for trails and the campground, and built several structures. The campground was established in 1934, by which time walking trails connected the three tallest dunes. Wilson and City West Shelters were built in 1935.

By the mid-1950s, attendance had skyrocketed. On hot summer weekends, the park often reached its visitor capacity, and officials would turn away cars at the entrance. This is no longer done, but

The crowd on the beach at Dunes State Park, 1955. The pavilion and Dunes Arcade Hotel can be seen at the left. *Arthur Anderson, Calumet Regional Archives*

when the park is at capacity now, arriving cars may be held up at the entrance and allowed in only as others leave.

More recent improvements include the Nature Center, which was built at the western edge of the nature preserve in 1990. In 2004–2005, two large and modern comfort stations were built at the campgrounds while the number of campsites was reduced from 293 to 140 in order to increase spacing and improve the camping experience. Interestingly, with no fee increases, camping revenues increased by 40 percent after the changes were made.

After being buried in a culvert for about seventy years, Dunes Creek was restored to an open-air channel in a multi-year project beginning in 2005. This action also created a wetland area that now filters the water and deters pollutants from entering the lake.

In the spring of 2007, ecologists and staff began the process of returning what had been a black oak savanna to its naturally open state. In order to do this, invasive species were removed, trees less than twenty years old were removed, and prescribed burns were implemented. As hoped, a diversity of prairie species populations emerged, including coreopsis, lupine, several sedges, and a rare grass species.

The investments have paid off. Indiana Dunes State Park has preserved much of the beauty of Duneland while becoming one of the most popular of all state parks in Indiana. After years of being a favorite vacation spot for Hoosiers, its attributes finally became recognized across the country when *Midwest Living* magazine in 2010 named the park one of the thirty-five best Midwestern state parks—a recognition that was repeated in 2011.

## *1929 Beverly Shores*

Beverly Shores is a lakeside community planned by Chicagoan Frederick Bartlett, who in 1927 purchased land east of Dunes State Park. His dream was an elegant resort community with easy access to Chicago via either the new Dunes Highway (US 12) or the South Shore Railroad. Bartlett designed several subdivisions, constructed access roads, and built two South Shore depots (the one on Broadway still standing) so that residents could easily commute to downtown Chicago or Hyde Park and other areas of southern Chicago. Chicagoans who preferred to live in the city were encouraged to build a second home at Beverly Shores so that they could get away for a weekend or a long summer vacation.

In keeping with the resort theme, Bartlett built an eighteen-hole golf course south of the entrance at Route 12 and chose a Mediterranean Revival style for the community's public buildings. These included the depots, the administration building, and even a service station on Route 12. He named the community for his niece Beverly—the daughter of his younger brother Robert.

The Administration Building, designed by Chicago architect Arthur Gerber and constructed in 1929 by the Leo W. Post Construction Company. *Beverly Shores Historical Society*

The Beverly Shores depot. Still in use.

The Armco-Ferro house being transported across the lake to Beverly Shores. *Beverly Shores Historical Society*

Lenard's Casino showing the hotel to the left. This was a restaurant (rather than a gaming facility) with a lower level having lockers and a refreshment stand on the beach. *Beverly Shores Historical Society*

2. Not a gambling institution. "Casino" comes from the Italian word for a summer or country house, which is similar to the Spanish word "casa."

On July 22, 1929, Frederick Bartlett announced through a full-page ad in the *Chicago Tribune* that he had 1,400 acres of prime land to be developed—the largest lakeshore development project in the greater Chicago region. Three months later, the stock market crashed. Intrigued investors purchased many lots during the first several years of the Depression, but few houses were built.

### 1933—A New Start

In 1933, Bartlett turned over the control of Beverly Shores to his brother Robert, who then redoubled efforts to both improve and market his development. A double row of trees was planted along Broadway, more streets were paved, and an impressive hotel and a theater were built. Robert even brought in the cast for stage plays from Chicago's Goodman Theater. Would-be buyers were enticed to ride the South Shore Railroad from Chicago to view this new resort community. Their efforts paid off: sixteen homes were built in 1933–34. Not bad for the Depression!

In 1934, Bartlett arranged for sixteen houses from Chicago's Century of Progress World's Fair to be brought to Beverly Shores. Four of them came across the lake by barge, and another twelve came by truck. Five of the houses were placed along Lake Front Drive. (See the section about the World's Fair Houses.) Others were spread out in the southern part of the development. Of this latter group, only the "Old North Church" still stands.

Also in 1934, Bartlett built a strikingly beautiful restaurant on the beach near Broadway. The building was constructed of sand-tan and sea-green terra cotta with jet-black trim. For its first three years, it was known as the Beverly Shores Casino.[2]

Starting in 1938, and for twenty-nine subsequent years, this well-known establishment was run by the family of Ignatz Lenard, a Polish Chicago restauranteur. Lenard added a hotel building to the west and made the facility a year-round lake-side resort. He renamed it Lenard's Casino.

The transplanted houses, Casino, and other buildings elicited a lot of publicity and much excitement, and Beverly Shores grew. Within a few years the town had many new homes, a post office, and a school.

In 1946, with the lots all sold, Bartlett turned over the roads and the administration building to the landowners. The next year, Beverly Shores was incorporated as a town.

## The Lithuanians

In the years that followed World War II, a number of families from Lithuania purchased homes in Beverly Shores. They apparently found the shoreline similar to the seacoast vacation spots of the Baltic. The Lithuanian community grew until it was about one quarter of the town's population, so large that a Lithuanian priest from Chicago started coming out monthly to St. Ann of the Dunes church to celebrate mass in Lithuanian. The Lakeside Villa, with its cottages and a lunchroom serving homemade Lithuanian foods, was run by Lithuanians J. Mildazis and Joe Cesna. In 1970, local Lithuanians donated the seven-acre Lithuanica Park to the town. The American-Lithuanian Club of Beverly Shores still marks Lithuania's independence each year on February 16 and also hosts an annual picnic in the Park.

## The Red Lantern Inn

In 1967, the Lenard family sold its "Casino" to Bill Dibulak, Jack Panozzo, and the Ruzioc family. They engaged Long Beach architect Ray Stuermer to redesign the building, and it re-opened in April of 1968 as the Red Lantern Inn. The new design included four dining and banquet areas, two lounges, twenty-five guest rooms, an apartment, and a penthouse. Its Lakeview Room could handle banquets for up to five hundred guests. The first banquet held there was a campaign dinner for presidential candidate Robert Kennedy. The principal speaker was Kennedy's mother, Rose.

The Red Lantern soon became a favorite place for prom dinners, banquets, and receptions. In 1971, the resort was purchased by the National Park Service, which then leased it to Roger Larson. His sons Kenny and Danny operated it until 1986, when the lease expired. A new fifteen-year lease was negotiated, but it would have required the Larsons to make improvements that the short length of the lease didn't justify. The Inn closed and was razed.

A road sign for the Lakeside Villa. Standing are owners Terese Mildazis and her mother Stefanija Cesna. *Beverly Shores Historical Society*

The Red Lantern Inn entrance on Lakefront Drive. *(below) Ken Larson*

The establishment in the 1960s of a national park caused great excitement and concern in Beverly Shores. Some favored the park; others did not. In the end, when the park boundaries were set in 1966, the town's most developed core was omitted. Many of the homeowners in the included section agreed to "Reservations of Use and Occupancy" whereby they accepted reduced prices for their properties and were then allowed to continue to live in them for twenty or more years.

Today Beverly Shores is a tight-knit community surrounded by the beauties of Lake Michigan and its dunes. Its population in 2010 was 613.

## 1933 *A Trip to the Dunes*

An inexpensive way for families and friends to spend the Fourth of July, even during the depths of the Great Depression, was a trip down the Dunes Highway to Dunes State Park.

The Pavilion was well equipped with showers, lockers, and changing rooms. Park visitors could either bring a picnic lunch or eat in the Pavilion's dining room.

It was quite popular for groups of young people to meet near the Pavilion and then hike in the woods, lounge on the beach, and enjoy the waters of Lake Michigan away from the noise of the city. The new campgrounds were available for those who could spend more than just one day. So, on Tuesday, July 4, 1933, not having to go to work, 23 year-old Michael N. Kobe and a bunch of friends headed off to Dunes State Park.

Preparing for the drive from North Hammond to Indiana Dunes State Park.
*All photos are by Michael N. Kobe.*

The Dunes Arcade Hotel, Pavilion, and parking lot from the top of the Devil's Slide. The view from the top has for years been worth the effort of the climb. *(left)*

Celebrating
July 4th

231

## 1941 *Good Fellow Youth Camp*

The Good Fellow Youth Camp opened on July 20, 1941, as a summer camp for the children of employees of Gary Works of the United States Steel Company.

For the next thirty-five years, kids aged eight to fifteen would come out to the camp for a week of fun and relaxation. Besides its playground with swings, a slide, and a merry-go-round, the camp had a large stainless steel swimming pool, tennis, handball, basketball, badminton, and shuffleboard courts, an archery range, and a croquet lawn.

Good Fellow Lodge with its original log exterior. *NPS*

The camp was run by the Gary Works Good Fellow Club, a social club open to all employees at the mill, both supervisors and laborers. It was open for eight weeks each summer and hosted sixty to a hundred children at a time. Steel mill officials believed that it was good for kids to get away from the noise and dirty air of the city and spend some time surrounded by field and forest near the shores of Lake Michigan.

The Good Fellow Lodge contained the dining hall and kitchen. When first built, it had a log exterior deliberately made to look rustic like the great lodges of Yellowstone or Glacier National Park. The two-story interior dining/assembly hall complemented the exterior, with its large stone fireplace and knotty cedar paneling. Here campers gathered before its massive flagstone fireplace for assemblies, sing-alongs, talent shows, and movies. Until 1951, both campers and counselors slept in canvas tents. At that time, they were replaced with cabins.

The stainless steel pool was built soon after the war. It was considered such a great example for showing the potential of stainless steel products that executives from the Pittsburgh headquarters came to the camp for the pool's dedication in 1946. That year, the *Gary Post Tribune* noted that the recently improved camp, with its handsome curved flagstone entrance, was "one of the best-equipped youth outing centers this side of the Adirondacks."

Camp director Vernon Charlson hangs the camp sign. *(top)*

A counselor leads a bunch of kids on a hike. *(above)*

Tents were used for sleeping in the early days. *(left)*

*All photos from the NPS collection*

The large lodge fireplace was the location of many skits, games, and conversations. *(right)*

The swimming pool, made of stainless steel, was a showpiece for US Steel. *(below)*

Until the 1960s, children of black employees attended during special weeks assigned to them. *(below right)*

*All photos from the NPS collection*

The campgrounds were west of the Bailly Homestead. The program staff took advantage of the location to emphasize the determination and positive outlook of American pioneers and the atmosphere of friendship that existed between them and the local Indian tribes. The Camp stressed Indian lore, nature study, local history, and handcrafts.

Attending Camp Good Fellow always meant more than a week of fun and games. The Good Fellow Club fully intended that campers learn the values of sportsmanship, etiquette, and appreciation for the outdoors. Camp staff used local pioneer and Native American stories to demonstrate a common heritage to campers who came from both privileged executive and immigrant laborer families. Fees were deliberately kept low ($4 a week in 1945), yet scholarships were still available for families with limited means. According to Charlson, the staff expected campers to forget their differences and perform duties equally.

As is often the case, a number of factors culminated in the decision to end the camping program. The growth of local parks and recreation programs gave parents more options for organized activities for their children. The gas crisis of 1973 and the economic recession were factors as well. In the mid-1970s, it was decided to close the camp. The last session ended in August of 1976.

In July of 1977, the National Park Service purchased the grounds. In the years since, the lodge building has had its roof replaced and has been made weathertight. Plans call for the building to be restored and used again.

# 1952 Port or Park: Dreams in Dissonance

## A Public Port on Lake Michigan

Plans to establish a public deepwater port on Lake Michigan predate Indiana's statehood. It was this early Hoosier dream that resulted in the state boundary line (today at Indian Boundary Road) being moved from the southern tip of Lake Michigan to a line ten miles north of that.

Fur trader Joseph Bailly planned for a Porter County port in the early 1830s. As noted elsewhere in this book, the citizens of City West in 1837 lobbied Daniel Webster for funds to build a port. The dredging of Burns Ditch in 1926 for flood relief sparked new efforts to create a public port. However, efforts stalled again once the Great Depression took hold.

In Porter County, Inland Steel owned a mile of lakefront between Miller and Ogden Dunes. Since 1929, Midwest Steel had owned 750 acres straddling Burns Ditch. Midwest executives and

George A. Nelson, a forty-year crusader for the port. *Courtesy of Nancy J. Douglass and Jane A. Holmgren*

many Porter County businessmen were hoping that the federal government would build a deepwater port at the ditch. But the Army Corps of Engineers in both 1931 and 1935 rejected that idea because it would benefit just that one company.

So businessmen, spearheaded by Valparaiso Chamber of Commerce manager, George Nelson, planned for a public port east of the Midwest properties and urged Congress to provide funding. Much of that land was owned by the Consumers Company of Chicago, a corporation that was already lobbying Congress for a port that would support heavy industry on the lakefront. Meanwhile, NIPSCO, which owned three hundred acres of land just west of Dune Acres, was waiting for the industrial development that would need the electricity that NIPSCO could provide. George Nelson was an articulate, well-respected, and persistent business leader who galvanized much support for the port.

Adding to the pressures for industrial development in the late 1950s was the impending opening of the St. Lawrence Seaway that would allow ocean-going vessels to come directly to ports on Lake Michigan. Even area farmers could imagine their harvest being shipped overseas to customers half a world away.

Meanwhile, a growing number of northwest Indiana residents were becoming alarmed at the prospect of the dunes being leveled. They had heard that some developers were referring to the Lake Michigan shoreline as an industrial crescent and that some even talked about having the state sell Dunes State Park. Even if that never were to happen, they could envision open space disappearing.

## Save the Dunes Council

So it happened that on June 20, 1952, twenty-one women gathered at the Ogden Dunes home of Dorothy Buell to listen to Bess Sheehan tell the story of her involvement and success in creating the state park thirty years earlier. The women then organized the Save the Dunes Council with the goal of reigniting the national park movement and preserving the natural lakeshore and dunelands.

Dorothy Buell was an amazing woman. As a child, she had visited the dunes and even participated in the great Duneland Pageant of 1917. In 1952, she was sixty-five years old, a time when many folks are thinking of slowing down. But Mrs. Buell had a dream.

Dorothy Buell, first president of the Save the Dunes Council. *Save the Dunes*

Speaking for the new organization, she announced, "We are prepared to spend the rest of our lives, if necessary, to save the Dunes."

She had what Herbert Read called "a commanding presence, combined with steely determination, dignity, enthusiasm, optimism, and the ability to attract people with the specific skills necessary to accomplish a task."

Sometimes, here in the twenty-first century, it's hard to imagine what these determined folks were up against. The environmental movement hadn't yet arrived. Folks didn't celebrate Earth Day. Wetlands were considered bad and unhealthy. And the federal government had not yet ever purchased land for a national park. (All the parks were federal properties that simply had never been sold.) Indiana government officials and elected congressmen and senators strongly favored industrial development.

Yet the need for more recreational lands was unmistakable. In the summer, Gary's Marquette Park and Michigan City's Washington Park were jam-packed. Dunes State Park was so overcrowded that on holidays or summer weekends the State Police had to turn away cars at the park entrance. Johnson's Beach in Porter sometimes had more than a thousand cars in its parking lot on hot July weekends.

Mrs. Buell started the effort to win over public opinion with dozens of speaking engagements. Photographer John Nelson produced a film describing the Dunes, which was shown to local clubs and service organizations. Members of many groups responded to the call for help. These efforts resulted in more than 250,000 persons signing a petition to preserve the dune landscape.

In those early days, it was hoped that the Council could raise enough money to purchase the Dunes. Indeed, when the area known as Cowles Bog was put on the market, the Council did raise the money to purchase that property. But Duneland was far too large for a small organization to be able to purchase the entire area with donated funds. Getting Congress to establish a park was also unlikely, as Indiana's governor and two senators favored the port.

The Central Dunes in 1962.
*Arthur Anderson,*
*Calumet Regional Archives*

## Dreams Delayed

With the prospect that a port would soon be built, Bethlehem Steel Company in 1955 purchased 1,200 acres of open duneland between Midwest Steel's property and Dune Acres.

As Representative Charlie Halleck and both of Indiana's US senators supported the port, Mrs. Buell contacted Illinois Senator Paul Douglas of Chicago. In his younger days, Senator Douglas had spent many enjoyable hours at the dunes, and he agreed to help. On May 26, 1958, as promised, he introduced a bill to establish a national park in the Dunes. At the Senate hearings in Washington, with sixty Save the Dunes Council members in the room and with the walls holding paintings of the Dunes by Frank Dudley (which the Council members had brought with them on their bus), Council members were informed that bulldozers had begun to level the land that they were trying to preserve. Sylvia Troy, who later served as president of the Save the Dunes Council, noted that this was the low point of the struggle and that the Council seriously considered giving up.

Stewart Udall, Secretary of the Interior; Senator Alan Bible, Chair of the Senate Interior Subcommittee; Senator Paul Douglas; and Conrad Wirth, director of the National Park Service, walk through dunes on land owned by Bethlehem Steel Company, July, 1961. In the background is the 150-foot dune known locally as "Howlin' Hill." *Calumet Regional Archives*

Fearing that delay would make building a plant impossible, Midwest Steel began construction of its mill in 1959—even though there was neither a port nor a decision by Congress to build one. The next year, NIPSCO began construction of its coal-fired Bailly Generating Station just west of Dune Acres. However, an Army Corps of Engineers feasibility study recommending a port was found to have errors, and the US Bureau of the Budget decided against endorsing the port and thus halted congressional approval.

Council members visited all 535 members of Congress. Slowly, the Council's efforts began to convince formerly skeptical citizens. Preservation was soon supported not only by environmental groups but also by area chambers of commerce, the League of Women Voters, unions, and service clubs. Representative Ray Madden told the Council that in his thirty years on the Hill, he had never before been lobbied by twenty-two groups on a single issue.

Local mayors join Dorothy Buell, Congressman Ray Madden, and Senator Paul Douglas as a show of support for the Save the Dunes movement. Left to right: Dorothy Buell, Representative Madden, George Chacharis of Gary, Richard J. Daley of Chicago, Walter Jeorse of East Chicago, Senator Douglas, Mary Bercik of Whiting, Senator Alan Bible, National Park Service Director Conrad Wirth, and Interior Secretary Stewart Udall. *Calumet Regional Archives*

In 1961, Mrs. Buell and Senator Douglas organized a highly publicized tour of the dunes for Interior Secretary Stewart Udall, National Park Service Director Conrad Wirth, and several area mayors. Indiana's rather new Senator Vance Hartke and soon-to-be Senator Birch Bayh came on board.

But by 1962, both dreams seemed thwarted. Neither the port nor the park proposals could get support from a majority of Congress. President Kennedy, who supported the park, proposed a compromise in which both the port and the park would be established. His assassination in 1963, however, doomed the prospects of an early resolution to the problem. Representative Charles Halleck from DeMotte, in whose district the port and park would be located, was the US House Minority Leader and a strong supporter of the port and the mills.

## Finally, an Agreement

President Lyndon Johnson, in his 1965 State of the Union address, declared that the country had too few parks, seashores, and recreational areas, and by name supported creating the Indiana Dunes National Lakeshore. In the end, an agreement was reached in Congress whereby industry, the port, and the Indiana Dunes

Save the Dunes Council member Judson Harris drives Senator Paul Douglas to a rally attended by both supporters and opponents of saving the dunes, July 23, 1961. Behind them are Chicago Mayor Richard J. Daley and Gary Mayor George Chacharis. *Calumet Regional Archives*

Save the Dunes Council members celebrate the Council's twentieth anniversary at the Red Lantern Inn, September, 1972. From left: Sylvia Troy, Harold Olin, Charlotte Read, Ed Osann, and Emily Taft (Mrs. Paul) Douglas. *Calumet Regional Archives*

National Lakeshore would share Indiana's shoreline. Final approval came in 1966. A few months later, the Port of Indiana held its official groundbreaking.

By this time, Midwest Steel had already opened. Bethlehem Steel opened in 1967. Soon, NIPSCO's Bailly Generating Station followed, and Indiana's International Port, now the Port of Indiana at Burns Harbor, was opened in 1969. George Nelson was honored by having the main street within the port area named for him.

The Indiana Dunes National Lakeshore was to protect eight miles of shore and 8,330 acres of parkland, including the State Park, which could be acquired only if the state decided to donate it.

With the park authorized, the Save the Dunes Council considered disbanding. However, it was soon discovered that Congress had not authorized any monies to purchase land, and so in 1967 another lobbying effort was required to secure acquisition funds. The Council's members soon realized that continuing diligence was needed, and so the Save the Dunes Council, now known simply as Save the Dunes, still works toward care and preservation of the Dunes.

## 1956 *The Enchanted Forest*

Going to the Enchanted Forest was once the dream of thousands of Duneland children. The Enchanted Forest was a thirty-three-acre amusement park located on US 20 near Indiana 49. It opened in 1956 and had rides and attractions including a carousel, the Mad Mouse roller coaster, "Dodgem" (bumper cars), the Scrambler, the Twister, the Helicopter, an aerial tram ride, and what was said to be the tallest Ferris wheel in Indiana. There were also trampolines, a fun house, a Go-Kart racetrack, a petting zoo, and dozens of other attractions. A miniature train with a track that went all around the wooded park took visitors on leisurely rides. New attractions were added from time to time, always highlighted by local advertising. When visitors got hungry, they could go to one of three restaurants.

View from the Ferris wheel showing the Twister and the petting zoo (upper left). *Calumet Regional Archives*

The miniature railroad at the Enchanted Forest—a great ride for little kids. *Calumet Regional Archives*

By the late 1980s, attendance was dwindling, and the park could no longer cover all its expenses. In 1990, the owner, Candace Giro, had to declare bankruptcy. The park did not open for the 1991 season, and in October of that year, the rides, buildings, and decorations were all sold at auction. According to the *Gary Post-Tribune*, a generation weaned on MTV and theme parks like Great America found the "Playground of the Dunes" a bit too quaint.

The land itself later was used for a different kind of amusement park when Splash Down Dunes opened four years later.

*See also: Splash Down Dunes*

## 1966 Creating a National Park

One of the first tracts of land to be purchased was Inland Steel's West Beach. With that land acquired, a small staff of seasonal park rangers was hired for the summer of 1969, and the National Lakeshore was opened for business. On hot weekends, more than two thousand folks came to use the beach and walk through the dunes. At the end of the summer, staff members recommended providing lifeguards, drinking fountains, portable washrooms, a trailer to serve as a visitor station, and some mechanized way of cleaning the beach. At the time, the rangers had to shovel and rake the sand, as well as collecting and hauling away dead fish and lake debris, by hand. Staff also suggested prohibiting alcohol.

Meanwhile, land acquisition picked up speed. By the end of the year, 766 primarily small parcels had been purchased. Most of the sellers who lived in houses being purchased took advantage of the Reservations of Use and Occupancy option and were allowed to remain in their homes for periods up to twenty-five years.

Finally, after four years, the new park acquired a superintendent when James Whitehouse was named to that position in October, 1970. A few months later, he and the acquisition office moved into the former Presbyterian Church of the Dunes on Kemil Road. Superintendent Whitehouse attended numerous public, environmental, and business community meetings so as to build support and begin the process of reconciliation among various groups.

Sylvia Troy, Dorothy Buell, and Superintendent James Whitehouse at the dedication of the new administration building, 1971. *Save the Dunes Collection, Calumet Regional Archives*

Superintendent Whitehouse was greatly assisted by the members of the Indiana Dunes National Lakeshore Advisory Commission, a group created by Congress when it established the Lakeshore. Although five of the first seven Commission members were originally opposed to the National Lakeshore, the group had the ear of the public and enthusiastically offered valuable advice to Mr. Whitehouse.

When it was proposed that a third regional airport be built near Chesterton, the Commission strongly voiced its opposition, saying that the airport would be damaging to both the state and national parks. Later, it urged a speedy purchase of the Bailly Homestead before more deterioration could occur. The Commission helped soften the opposition to the park because it was composed of people who were respected by park opponents. Its input was so valuable that when it was to have expired in 1976, its authorization was extended for another five years.

The National Park Service's acquisition of the Bailly Homestead in 1971 was supported by historians, environmentalists, and the business community. At that time, no one knew whether the main house or the log structures were historically accurate or, if so,

The former Presbyterian Church on Kemil Road (Furnessville), used temporarily as park headquarters and then as the Dorothy Buell Visitor Center until the new Center was opened in 2006. *NPS*

whether they could be restored. The buildings were filthy and inhabited by squatters, their dogs, and their goats. Area citizens did know that the site of northwest Indiana's first European settlement and last Indian trading post was at least known to be an important part of the dunes and of Indiana's cultural heritage.

Also that year, a team including university faculty and Save the Dunes Council representatives explored all the units of the lakeshore with Superintendent Whitehouse, looking for ways to utilize the area's beauty without harming the fragile dunes ecosystem.

The Save the Dunes Council emphasized, and Nathaniel Reed, President Nixon's Assistant Secretary of the Interior, agreed, that the Indiana Dunes ecosystem was too fragile to be developed as a recreation area. Recreation areas would be developed primarily along the beach—and that for swimming and picnicking only. The remainder of the Lakeshore, Reed noted, would be disturbed only by trails. Hikers would then get a serene and inspiring experience.

## Dedication/Establishment Day, September 8, 1972

Six years after Congressional authorization, Indiana Dunes National Lakeshore was formally dedicated and ceremonially "established" on September 8, 1972. The ceremony, held at Dunes State Park, was attended by Interior Secretary Rogers Morton, Governor Edgar Whitcomb, and, representing her father, Julie Nixon Eisenhower. Although there had up to that point been discord between those who favored and those who opposed the park, on that day, Democrats and Republicans, businessmen and environmentalists, celebrated its existence.

Secretary Morton described the Dunes as "one of the crown jewels" of the President's parks program, calling it "a peaceful respite for ten million Americans who live and work nearby." Referring to the fifty-year effort to save the Dunes, he called the park a "lasting tribute to Senator Douglas's efforts."

## Interpretation

The park's first extensive interpretation program began in 1973. Up until that year, seasonal interpreter Darryl Blink gave occasional presentations at the Good Fellow Club and at Dunes State Park. That year, four additional seasonal interpreters were hired to give regularly scheduled summer presentations to park visitors. The number of visitors at programs jumped from 531 the year before to 2,571. The next year, the program was expanded to off-season visitors, focusing largely on school groups visiting the Dunes on one-day field trips. The interpretive schedule since then has spanned all twelve months of the year.

The other major event of 1973 was the unveiling of the National Park Service's Development Concept Plan for West Beach, which was done without any local input or public review. This audacious plan proposed twenty-six facilities for the area, including two swimming pools and steel bathhouses, a three-story parking garage for two thousand cars, a pavilion, sports fields, an amphitheater, sixteen homes for National Park Service employees, and maintenance and administration buildings. Save the Dunes Council members as well as the park's advisory commission members were shocked. They were angered, not only at the proposed over-development of the land but also at being shut out of the planning process. At a public hearing in Portage, every person who spoke condemned the plan. Several accused the National Park Service of high-handedness and going against the intent of Congress when the park was created. The Park Service not only withdrew the plans but changed its national policy to accommodate public review during rather than after the formulation of plans. Two years later, a single, but still grand, bathhouse, with showers, lockers, and food service, a six-hundred-car parking lot, and an entrance road were built. The bathhouse was dedicated on May 21, 1977.

The bathhouse at West Beach, the National Lakeshore's first recreational facility. *Kim Swift*

In 1974, the US Army announced plans to deactivate its NIKE missile base on Mineral Springs Road. As the headquarters and Visitor Center on Kemil Road had become cramped, it was agreed that the NIKE facility would nicely serve as a more comfortable and efficient headquarters for the National Lakeshore. The large

Bailly house before reconstruction, circa 1975. *NPS*

facility was an ideally centrally located place from which to conduct Lakeshore operations.

The old Visitor Center and the Bailly Administrative Area are both examples of adaptive reuse of existing facilities. Almost all the park's new developments have been placed on previously disturbed lands. There were buildings at the Kemil Beach parking lot and the Glenwood Dunes Trail; Dunewood Campground is where the Beverly Shores golf course had been. Placing developments in already disturbed areas preserved untouched duneland.

In 1976, restoration activities began at the Bailly Homestead. An historic structure report had suggested that the historic period for the log outbuildings would be the 1820s—about the time they were first built—while the main house would be restored to its appearance in 1917, the last year members of the Bailly family had lived there. The exterior of the Bailly house was completed in time for an American Bicentennial–flavored dedication on July 11—an event attended by more than 250 people.

In 1976, after years of proposals, debates, and committee hearings, and almost as a memorial to the recently deceased former Senator Paul Douglas, Congress approved a 4,205-acre expansion of the National Lakeshore. Much of the land had been included in the boundaries that were suggested by President Kennedy but deleted before the 1966 authorization. The areas added to the park included the Crescent Dune, Heron Rookery, Inland Marsh, Miller Woods, Tolleston Dunes, and two miles of the Little Calumet River in Porter County.

In the banner year of 1978, the park and the Westchester Public Library helped sponsor the Duneland Folk Festival at the newly restored Bailly Homestead. The festival included traditional crafts, music, and dancing. That year, the first edition of the *Singing Sands Almanac,* the park's newsletter, was published. The Almanac had a dramatic impact on Lakeshore operations. It gave the park a higher profile and informed the community about programs and special events. The number of visitors to the park that year surpassed the one million mark for the first time.

The next year, Maple Sugar Time and Autumn Harvest programs were established at the Chellberg Farm. The latter exceeded expectations when it brought more than a thousand visitors to the park in just one day. (In 1980, the program was extended to two days and brought in three thousand visitors.) In 1985, it merged with the Duneland Folk Festival and was renamed the Duneland Harvest Festival. In 2009, it became Duneland Heritage Days. The environmental education programs, especially for area schools, were becoming an established part of the curriculum for many local school districts: more than 33,000 students came every year.

In 1979, Michigan City donated Mount Baldy to the National Lakeshore. And then in 1980, Congress added another 480 acres to the park, including an addition to Miller Woods and the campgrounds in Porter County.

For many years, volunteers had played an important part in park programming. In July of 1982, many of these volunteers organized the "Friends of the Indiana Dunes," a non-profit group dedicated to enhancing and fostering understanding, appreciation, and enjoyment of the Indiana Dunes through financial and volunteer support. Within just a few years, this group had become a 501(c)(3) organization, which allowed it to apply for and receive grants and tax-deductible gifts, and was sponsoring or assisting with many special events.

After twelve years at the Lakeshore, Superintendent Whitehouse retired in October, 1982, and was succeeded by Assistant Superintendent Dale Engquist. That year, because of a new federal policy, the Lakeshore had to stop publishing the *Singing Sands Almanac.* But after a hiatus of just three years, the Friends of the Indiana Dunes group revived the newsletter by selling subscriptions. Ten dollars bought a year-long subscription as well as a membership in the organization. Glenda Daniel became the Almanac's editor.

In the 1980s, the Lakeshore solidified its position in Northwest Indiana as the old animosity between environmentalists and industrialists began to disappear. Nearly all residents by then valued having world-famous beaches and a national park in "their own backyard." Volunteers from the various nearby communities helped organize programs and in doing so helped strengthen relationships between their communities and the park.

Our relations with the Save the Dunes Council are very good. We have regular communications. They are generally good. We're generally mutually supportive. We have an ultimate goal that's the same. We differ sometimes on methods and procedures and we don't always agree on everything. I view them, personally, kind of as my conscience. I'd like to think I'd always keep uppermost in my mind the preservation goals for Indiana Dunes National Lakeshore. With the Save the Dunes Council out there, you can be assured that should you ever think of straying from the pure path you will be quickly reminded!

—SUPERINTENDENT DALE ENGQUIST,
*Indiana Dunes National Lakeshore,*
*September 16, 1987*

Dale Engquist, Superintendent, 1982-2007. *NPS*

## The 1986 Expansion Bill

In 1985, the Save the Dunes Council worked with fairly new Congressman Peter J. Visclosky of Indiana to put together a viable expansion bill, which was introduced in the House of Representatives in January, 1986. In September, Senators Danforth Quayle and Richard Lugar introduced a parallel bill in the Senate. With uncharacteristic speed, both houses concurred on an amended measure in October. President Reagan signed the bill, and more than nine hundred acres were added to the Lakeshore.

The new land additions rounded out some of the park's boundaries. The bill included what is now the Calumet Trail and the NIPSCO/South Shore Railroad corridor, but it prevented the National Park Service from acquiring that land while it was still in use. In addition, segments of the Little Calumet River and Salt Creek were incorporated to continue efforts to connect the east and west units of the park.

## Paul H. Douglas Center for Environmental Education

Congress authorized the Paul H. Douglas Center for Environmental Education in 1980. It was designed in 1984 (using input from students), built just west of Lake Street in Miller Woods, and dedicated September 14, 1986. The large building included kid-friendly exhibits, assembly rooms, and lab space. The Center and the trails that go out from it have served thousands of students and teachers in the years since. With it, environmental education programs grew by 11 percent in the first year to thirty-four thousand participants. The general non-school programs served another thirty thousand persons.

US Representative Peter Visclosky and Gary Mayor Richard Hatcher talk with students before the official ribbon cutting at the Paul H. Douglas Center for Environmental Education at Miller Woods. *(facing above)*

Area students help Dr. Mark Reshkin, chair of the Friends of the Indiana Dunes, and William Penn Mott, director of the National Park Service, cut the ribbon at the Douglas Center dedication. *(facing inset)*
*Both photos courtesy of Save the Dunes*

# 1970 *The Battle over Bailly I*

The Battle over Bailly I is an example of what can happen when dreams conflict. The dream of NIPSCO was to construct a modern nuclear generating station on its property along the Lake Michigan shoreline. Its opponents' dreams were quite different.

In the late 1960s, when the National Park and port were quite new, the chairman and board of directors of the Northern Indiana Public Service Company (NIPSCO) decided to move forward on plans to construct a nuclear-powered generating station, Bailly I, on its property next to its still rather new coal-fired Bailly Generating Station. In 1970, NIPSCO submitted its application to the Licensing Board of the Atomic Energy Commission. It estimated the construction costs at less than $108,000,000.

The concern was location.

Bailly I was to be located south of Lake Michigan, between Bethlehem Steel and the town of Dune Acres. The executives of NIPSCO particularly liked the site because it would have access to Lake Michigan water for cooling and was conveniently close to the company's biggest customers, the new and not-so-new steel mills along the Lake Michigan Shoreline. Opponents particularly disliked the proposed site because it was right next to both populated areas and Cowles Bog, a fragile ecosystem that was an American Natural Landmark and part of the new National Lakeshore.

The news, however, was met with approval by many of the businesses in the area and probably a majority of the citizens of and near Duneland. Conservationists, many of them members of the Porter County Chapter of the Izaak Walton League, were concerned that Cowles Bog might be destroyed and that the two ten-story-high cooling towers would dominate the view around the national park. Others objected to the plan as they believed nuclear energy to be unsafe and didn't believe that the mills and residential neighborhoods could be easily evacuated in case of an emergency.

While NIPSCO completed plans for its facility, opponents conferred, organized, studied their options, and prepared to speak at the public hearings scheduled to begin in October, 1972, in Gary.

Dune Acres was clearly the residential community most affected by the plans. In January of 1972, a group of residents formed the

"Concerned Citizens Against the Bailly Nuclear Site." James New-man, professor of history at IU Northwest, and attorney Edward Osann were elected as co-chairs of the group. Ed also served as the group's attorney, doing much work for no charge and the rest for just 25 percent of his normal rate. At a preliminary hearing on May 9, 1972, the Concerned Citizens, the Izaak Walton League, and four individuals—George Hanks, IUN professor of biology, Ed Osann, an engineer and attorney, Mildred Warner, and Jim Newman—were accepted as intervenors. Referred to as "joint intervenors," they not only could speak at the hearings but also had the right to call witnesses. Opposing the nuclear plant would be expensive, and the Concerned Citizens group knew that it would have to raise more than $25,000, much of which initially came from residents of the town. Other donors were the Save the Dunes Council and the Izaak Walton League. In the end, the costs escalated to more than $150,000.

The Concerned Citizens did not picket or hold rallies because, as Dr. Newman noted, "it would have been useless." Nuclear power at that time was popular, and most northwest Indiana residents seemed to support NIPSCO's plans. Indeed, Newman found that "public reaction to us was fairly hostile." Folks believed that with nuclear power, electric bills would go down.

Cowles Bog was at the center of the environmental concerns both because its chemical balance was delicate and because it was so close to the proposed reactor site. There was grave concern about changes in the ground water and acid mists that might form around the cooling towers. Scientists from Purdue and the University of Chicago testified at the hearings and emphasized that both the construction and the operation of the nuclear plant could damage the wetland.

The public hearings dragged on for sixty-five days, over thirteen months' time—the longest hearings up to that time on a nuclear plant application. When they concluded in November of 1973, more than a hundred witnesses had given testimony and there were more than ten thousand pages of transcripts recording the proceedings. The joint intervenors felt good after the hearings and so were greatly disappointed when, the following April, NIPSCO-received its license to build its Bailly I reactor. Concerning Cowles

Bog, NIPSCO was told to monitor the area and fix damage if it occurred.

The joint intervenors quickly reviewed the decision and appealed the decision to the Atomic Safety and Licensing Appeal Board, but not surprisingly that board also ruled against them. Then NIPSCO started construction, even though by that time the projected cost of the plant had more than doubled to $243,000,000.

Disappointed, the joint intervenors filed an appeal with the US Court of Appeals on September 13, 1974. The team was joined at this stage by the state of Illinois and Michael Swygert representing the city of Gary. Bob Vollen, a member of the Chicago-based public interest law firm of Business People for the Public Interest, also joined the team and coordinated many of the legal efforts.

This time the team was successful. The court ruled in its favor on April 1, 1975, and for the first time in US history, a court halted the construction of an approved nuclear power plant. The issue in the courts was not whether a nuclear power plant should be built but whether the AEC had followed its own policies. A major point of contention was how to measure the distance from the proposed reactor to the nearest major population center.

The Appeals Court claimed that the AEC was wrong in approving the license for construction of the plant because it had violated its own rule concerning the required distance between such a plant and the boundaries of nearby cities. It also affirmed an earlier stop order ordering NIPSCO not to dewater the site. Finally, it ordered the excavation to be filled.

By 1974, the AEC's regulatory programs had come under such strong attack that Congress abolished the agency, replacing it with the Nuclear Regulatory Commission (NRC). What followed the apparent 1975 victory for the joint intervenors was reversed in a series of hearings.

- July 1, 1975: NIPSCO (with NRC support) appealed to the US Supreme Court.
- Nov. 11, 1975: The Supreme Court, deferring to "administrative expertise," agreed with the AEC's own interpretation of its rules and reversed the Appeals Court decision. It also remanded the entire case back to the Appeals Court.

- Apr. 13, 1976: The Appeals Court reviewed the case, changed its position, and unanimously ruled in favor of NIPSCO.
- Aug. 27, 1976: The joint intervenors petitioned the US Supreme Court to review that decision.
- Nov. 8, 1976: The US Supreme Court denied the joint intervenors' petition.
- After the court decisions were handed down, NIPSCO resumed construction in spite of the fact that a reconfiguration of the project cost projected the final bill to be about $705,000,000— more than six times the original cost estimate.

Soon after NIPSCO restarted work on the project, it was discovered that they could not get the pilings as deep as their permit required. In spite of the objections of the Concerned Citizens group, the Nuclear Regulatory Commission approved shorter pilings but NIPSCO had additional problems with them and construction had to stop in 1977.

## The Opposition Expands

In 1977, the opposition to the proposed nuclear reactor started to grow dramatically. A new organization, the Bailly Alliance, was organized that year. Its mission was to "spread the word," popularize the efforts to stop construction of the reactor, and organize rallies and public protests. Its first rally was held in Chesterton in November of 1977. The Bailly Alliance eventually had nine chapters in northern Indiana.

Then in June of 1978, reacting to the nearness of the proposed plant to the steel mills of Porter County, District 31 of the United Steelworkers of America voted to oppose construction of the nuclear reactor. In addition to the dangers of an accident, the union noted the unsolved problems of nuclear waste, constant low-level radiation, and the rapidly escalating costs of building nuclear plants.

A huge concern of steel workers was that if the mill ever had to be evacuated, dozens of men would have to remain for at least three days to properly shut down the furnaces. Just three months earlier, NIPSCO had revised the projected cost of building the reactor from $705,000,000 to $850,000,000.

253

"Better active today than radioactive tomorrow."
One of the more interesting slogans used by Bailly
Alliance protesters. *Calumet Regional Archives*

Bailly Alliance Rally, 1981.

The accident at Pennsylvania's Three Mile Island nuclear reactor on March 28, 1979, galvanized the anti-Bailly movement. At a June 1979 Alliance rally at Washington Park, union officials and community members denounced the reactor plans on both safety and economic grounds. They noted that nuclear power was becoming the most expensive way to generate electricity. In October, NIPSCO revised the cost estimate of the project to over a billion dollars ($1,100,000,000).

New concerns were raised as to whether Cowles Bog could survive the dewatering of the nearby reactor area. The National Lakeshore assembled a team of ground water experts to report on the environmental impact of the nearby construction. They discovered that the bog was directly connected by a sandy aquifer with the Bailly I reactor area and that draining the area would kill the bog. In fact, vegetation at the western edge of the bog was already dying. Interior Secretary Cecil Andrus asked the NRC to prepare a supplemental environmental impact statement.

Support for the anti-Bailly movement grew. Congressman Adam Benjamin, up to that point a supporter of the project, began to question it. The *Chesterton Tribune* denounced the proceedings of the Advisory Committee on Reactor Safeguards, which prohibited members of the public from asking questions at its hearings. Even the union representing NIPSCO workers opposed it.

On April 25, 1981, about two thousand "sign-carrying, slogan-chanting" demonstrators marched to the Bailly plant and released hundreds of balloons in what the Alliance called a "colorful way of illustrating an ugly fact." The next week, the *Gary Post-Tribune* came out against the reactor. Later that month, NIPSCO revised its cost estimate of the project to $1,815,000,000.

In August of that year, the NRC prohibited NIPSCO from resuming construction of its pilings until new hearings were held. Five days later, because of the huge cost of continuing, the company's board of directors voted to cancel the project.

# 1994 *Splash Down Dunes*

Splash Down Dunes, a grand water park, was built in 1994 on the grounds of the former Enchanted Forest in Porter. It had a wave pool, a lazy river, and up to thirteen different fun-filled water slides. The park was then said to be the largest water park in Indiana.

Among the attractions added later were the American Revolution, a forty-seven-foot-high ride consisting of a section that sent riders swirling around a giant bowl before sending them into a pool, and the Boomerango, which shot riders through a tunnel and up a hill before sliding them through a water curtain at the end.

The forty-three-foot-high Giant Twister featured four slides that took riders through multiple twists and turns. Riders were sent through multiple turns and dips before splashing into a refreshing pool.

The tallest structure, in fact the tallest water slide in the state, was the sixty-eight-foot steel Tower, which took riders over humps and dropped them at high speed into a pool below. It was said to be the perfect adrenaline rush for adults and older children seeking a thrilling ride.

The thirty-thousand-square-foot Big Wave was the largest wave pool in the Midwest. Guests could either use tubes or try to stand erect when the big waves raced across the pool.

Guests needing a break could meander down the Lazy River lying in a big tube on a slow, uneventful, relaxing 1,200-foot long "river." Those who enjoyed riding in tubes could also go down the twenty-nine-second Black Cobra tube slides, either in complete darkness or in an open-air river ride. Most kids wanted to do it both ways.

Splash Down Dunes also had areas for small children. Sandcastle Bay had a wading pool and three small water slides especially for the little folk. As its name suggested, there was plenty of sand for creating sculptures.

The park had a picnic area where guests could either purchase food or eat what they had brought from home. All in all, it was a great place to spend the day. The park closed at the end of the 2009 season because of an ownership dispute. It was sold in 2012 and plans were made to reopen the water park in 2013.

Splash Down Dunes with the wave pool in the foreground (and below), and the Black Cobra tube slides at the upper left. *Photos courtesy of Paul Childress*

# 1998 Dunes Learning Center

*From an essay by Lee Botts*

Since 1998 when it was established, the Dunes Learning Center has served more than sixty-five thousand students. Many of these children spent their first night away from home at the Center. Nearly all of them saw their first hawk, heard their first frog, identified their first tree, or had their first in-depth discussions about the environment there. Others first learned about food waste, energy savings, deer populations, sustainability, and shoreline erosion. For some local students, their days at the Center gave them their first view of Lake Michigan.

## An Education Mission

The National Lakeshore was established in 1966. When by 1968 no education programs had been established, the Save the Dunes Council contacted Lee Botts at Chicago's Openlands Project.

The result was the Lakeshore's first environmental education program—a free teacher workshop taught by Chicago science teacher Wayne Schimpf. This successful session resulted in the establishment of ongoing education programs that have made the Lakeshore an influential leader of environmental education within the National Park Service. A home converted into a center for education programs was used for many years until the Paul H. Douglas Center for Environmental Education was opened in 1986.

Yet Mrs. Botts and Mark Reshkin, later the Lakeshore's Chief Scientist, had long held a dream of establishing a residential environmental center similar to one that had recently been established at Yosemite. Only in a several-day residential format would there be enough time for children to see firsthand the area's various habitats and have in-depth discussions of ecosystems and sustainability. Superintendent Dale Engquist supported such a program, but to establish such a center would require authorization and support from Congress.

After a series of proposals, Congress approved the creation of a residential environmental education center in 1997. In a bill spon-

Dunes Learning Center's entrance sign on Howe Road.

sored by Representative Peter Visclosky and Senator Richard Lugar, Congress appropriated $750,000 for the creation of a residential environmental education center adjacent to the former Camp Good Fellow. Congress also approved an increase of $400,000 to the basic annual operating budget of the National Lakeshore for its operation.

## Creation of a Public/Private Partnership

To determine the best way of operating the center, members of Save the Dunes Council, Shirley Heinze Environmental Fund, and Friends of the Indiana Dunes met with teachers and staff from the National, State, and Lake County Parks. It was agreed that the aim should be providing residential programs primarily for school groups and that a new not-for-profit entity would be needed to serve as the necessary partner for the National Lakeshore.

In May of 1998, steps were taken to form a 501(c)(3) organization that would allow contributions to be tax deductible, and members were recruited for a board of directors. Knowing that the effort would require broad community support, it was decided to seek a balance of educators, environmental advocates, and business representatives on the board. Finally, it was decided to call the new facility the Indiana Dunes Environmental Learning Center, later shortened to Dunes Learning Center. Donated funds would be sought to keep fees as low as possible and to make the programs accessible to all schools—including those in areas where families couldn't afford to pay full program fees.

The first financial contribution, $15,000, was gratefully received from NiSource and made possible the immediate hiring of staff and establishment of an office. A logo designed by artist Mitch Markovitz was used for a letterhead and marketing materials.

## Physical Facilities

The Center's facilities include ten cabins, each with four bunk beds and separate toilet and shower rooms. Oversized bunk beds allow comfortable adult use. The cabins are grouped around a central open space used for gatherings and games.

The lodge building, with its dining/meeting area and kitchen, provides space for use in bad weather. A wide porch on two sides provides additional shelter. A short path leads to the campfire ring

The cabin interior with full-sized bunk beds that accommodate both adults and kids.

257

Construction of the cabins and lodge was done by National Park staff as time allowed. *NPS*

Lee Botts listens as a Nobel student describes her experiences at the first Frog In the Bog program. *Dunes Learning Center*

used in the evenings for singing, games that reinforce learning, and the roasting of "s'mores."

Construction of the cabins and lodge was slow because, to reduce costs, all but one of the structures were built by the National Park's maintenance staff as time was available. One cabin was built by industrial arts students from Portage High School.

## Getting Started

Matthew Miller was hired as the first executive director and served in that position for three years. Elma Thiele was recruited to work with a program committee and write a hands-on inquiry-based curriculum for fourth to sixth grade classes. The adopted program focuses on direct observation and analysis of relationships within natural and altered ecosystems.

The curriculum, named "Frog in the Bog," was designed to meet school standards in social studies, mathematics, language, and fine arts as well as science. It is a two-and-a-half-day program that includes an all-day hike on the Cowles Bog Trail with lunch and activities on the beach.

By April of 1998, the curriculum was ready to be tested with a fourth-grade class from Hammond. It was a chilly day with a penetrating mist. The hike on the Cowles Bog Trail was led by Learning Center/Park Service liaison Kim Swift. A surprise came later when students were asked what they had liked best and should be kept in the program. The most common response was "keep the rain." Further questioning revealed that being outside in the rain had been an exciting first-time experience that was enjoyable for all participants except the adults. This reinforced the intention to carry out most program activities outside in all but the most inclement or dangerous weather.

The grand opening of the Learning Center took place on Friday, October 9, 1998, at the end of the first week of operation. The first school group to participate (Monday–Wednesday) was a fourth-grade class from Gary's Nobel School. The second was from Jackson Township near Chesterton (Wednesday–Friday). Tom Serynek, the Nobel teacher, and his students returned on Friday to join in the formal ribbon cutting ceremony. Since that day, more than sixty-five thousand participants have been through the Dunes Learning Center programs.

## Growing

One unexpected problem was the fact that it was difficult to schedule groups for certain times of the year, particularly in the months of December through February. When John Hayes was hired as Executive Director in 2003, one of his biggest challenges was increasing participation, particularly in those months. Two new programs were developed, one for Science Olympiad participants and the other a winter survival program. Over time, the popularity of winter activities has grown. Some teachers prefer this time of year because it provides unique outdoor experiences. Hikes may be carried out on snowshoes or cross-country skis, and a campfire with snow all around is even more exciting than hiking in the rain.

A host of summer programs include Earth Camp, a program for East Chicago students, and Dunes Discovery Camp. Mighty Acorns is a program taught by Learning Center staff in school classrooms. The Dunes Learning Center has operated the Mighty Acorns outreach program since it was started by the Chicago Wilderness Consortium. The program, developed by Chicago's Field Museum, involves fourth-grade classes in restoring natural areas around their own neighborhoods. Learning Center staff goes out to the schools and works with the students there and at their chosen restoration area. The Learning Center's summer schedule includes two weeks of camp for Mighty Acorns participants.

Executive Director Matthew Miller, far left, and Garry Traynham, Lakeshore deputy superintendent, far right, assist as students cut the ribbon formally opening the Dunes Learning Center. *Dunes Learning Center*

# 2009 BioBlitz

## A National Geographic Project

A BioBlitz is a well-organized, fast-paced twenty-four-hour event in which students, teachers, and other community members team up with park rangers and volunteer scientists to find and identify as many species of living plants, animals, and other organisms as they can.

The National Geographic Society decided to hold a BioBlitz at a different national park each year from 2007 up until the National Park Service's centennial in 2016. The 2009 Blitz was at the Indiana Dunes National Lakeshore, where in spite of heavy rains more than 1,200 species were identified.

On May 15 and 16, the park hosted more than two thousand students and thousands of additional volunteers, who spread out in small groups and surveyed the park looking for every available living species they could find. The tally at the end of the search period was 890, but it grew to more than 1,200 after biologists had time to examine some species in their labs, confirm IDs, and compare notes.

Superintendent Constantine Dillon welcomed and thanked the volunteers. *(facing left) NPS, Lee Traynham*

Volunteers, including hundreds of students from area schools, came ready to work. *(facing right) NPS, Jeff Manuszak*

Volunteers planned the operation on land. *(facing below) NPS, James Beversdorf*

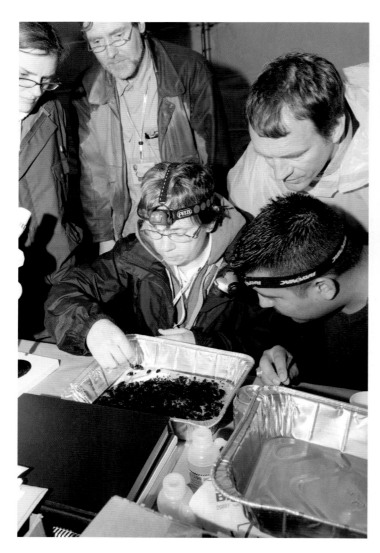

They used teamwork and expert help to identify species. *NPS, Bridget Sullivan*

They divided into teams to continue the search. *NPS, John Roquet*

Staff and volunteers shared discoveries as they were found. *NPS, Bridget Sullivan*

At their temporary headquarters, volunteers confirmed identifications, recorded data, and added up the numbers. *NPS, Lee Traynham*

## Ongoing Restoration: More Dreams Coming True

Environmental restoration activities in Duneland are ongoing and have been active for many decades. Restoration takes many forms, from simple cleanups, removal of invasive species, planting, and care of native species to removing ditches and drain tiles from previously drained wetlands.

The state of Indiana began a major restoration process at Dunes State Park when it was created in the 1920s. The National Park Service did the same when the National Lakeshore was established. The Indiana Department of Natural Resources, especially through its Heritage Trust license plate program, has raised and used voluntary contributions for hundreds of restoration purposes—many of them in Duneland.

Non-governmental organizations have done a vast amount of restoration work in Duneland. Organizations such as the Nature Conservancy, the Izaak Walton League, Save the Dunes, the Shirley Heinze Land Trust, Wildlife Habitat Council, and many others have restored or supported the restoration of thousands of acres of woodland, wetland, and prairie.

Local industries, park districts, schools, Scouts and other youth groups, and private landowners have done the same. All these efforts show how much business, industry, and local citizens care about the greater environment. They too have dreams for Duneland.

The following are just a few of the many projects of the last several years, starting with a company whose good works have outlived the company itself.

## Butterfly Habitat

When Midwest Steel needed to create a new landfill in 1992, the desired location was a field that contained lupine plants and the endangered Karner blue butterfly, whose larvae eat only lupine. So the company (in cooperation with the EPA) transplanted more than 1,600 of the plants and placed them on company property near the National Lakeshore. Crews then planted 7,900 lupine seeds and more than three thousand other native plants, and in addition, the company voluntarily purchased and set aside an additional fifty acres of good butterfly habitat.

## Little Calumet River Cleanup

Members of the Green Jobs Crew (laid-off steelworkers being retrained with ecological restoration skills) worked with Steward-ship Committee volunteers of the Northwest Indiana Paddling Association and town of Porter staff to clear a two-mile stretch of the Little Calumet River in the town of Porter.

Clearing the Little Calumet of limbs and other debris. *Northwest Indiana Paddling Association*

## Portage Lakefront and Riverwalk

The land west of the mouth of the Burns Waterway was optimistically added to the National Lakeshore in 1976. At that time, it was the site of the waste treatment plant and acid settling ponds of the National Steel Company. The transformation required partnerships and a special coordination of efforts.

The process included removal of hazardous materials from two settling lagoons used by National Steel and the agreement of the company to go beyond legal requirements to meet cleanup standards for the planned public use of the area. Much of this work was carried out by the plant's current owner, US Steel.

Portage Lakefront and Riverwalk, a restored industrial area.

The award-winning pavilion.

The site is part of Indiana Dunes National Lakeshore and was the first of several lakeshore projects that received funding from Northwest Indiana's Regional Development Authority (RDA). The site was dedicated in late 2008 and soon was drawing 150,000 visitors a year. At the dedication, Congressman Peter Visclosky called the park the linchpin of his Marquette Plan—a multi-year plan to increase public access to the Lake Michigan Shoreline.

The pavilion, perched on a dune bluff overlooking Lake Michigan and Burns Waterway, was designed by Design Organization to be a sustainable signature on the lakefront. Its design includes a series of metaphors: the roof reflects the curving forms of dunes and waves, the wooden soffit the hull of a boat, and the fireplace hearth and home.

The facility was awarded "LEED Gold Certification," as it includes reflective roofing, water and energy efficiency, the use of recycled and local materials, and a window glass pattern visible to birds.

In 2009, the site was named Indiana's "Outstanding Park Development" by the Indiana Parks and Recreation Association.

## Dunes Creek Daylighting

Back in the late 1920s, Dunes Creek was moved into a culvert and paved over. In an ambitious multi-year project beginning in 2005, the paving, fill, and pipes were removed and the creek restored to a natural look. In doing so, wetlands were created that now filter and deter pollutants from entering the lake.

An interesting partnership between the Indiana Department of Natural Resources and the Indiana Department of Correction resulted in minimum-security inmates from the Indiana State Prison at Michigan City doing some of the work to restore areas at Indiana Dunes State Park. They provided labor for projects that the state park just couldn't fund, including clearing salvage logs that were piled up in an area larger than half an acre. Another project involved removing invasive plants from an area at which Dunes Creek had just been "liberated" from its old culvert.

Dunes Creek toward the end of the daylighting project, 2011.

## Great Marsh Restoration

Wetlands were quite common in northwest Indiana 150 years ago. The lowlands south of the Tolleston Shoreline and north of the Calumet Shoreline then had plenty of water and a great diversity of plants and animals from LaPorte County westward to Illinois. In 1850, Congress passed the Swamp Land Act, which gave federal wetlands to the states in order to have them drained and made suitable for farming. It wasn't until 1972 that Congress reversed this itself by passing the Wetland Protection Act.

By this time, people had come to realize the value of wetlands.

The Great Marsh north of Route 12 in eastern Porter County was part of this extensive wetland. During the past hundred years, levees and ditches have altered its landscape, and the Great Marsh has shrunk in size. Ditching lowered the water table, and parts of the wetland became drier (which, of course, was the intent of the ditch diggers). This then reduced the habitat for waterfowl.

In 1998, the National Lakeshore began the process of restoring the Derby Ditch section of the marsh in Beverly Shores. Restoration activities have including plugging unneeded culverts and refilling ditches, removing non-native trees, and planting native plants. Scouts, area business employees, and students at Campagna Academy have all helped staff in this project.

There is still much to be done, but already flocks of mallard and wood ducks, great egrets, great blue and green herons, and even beaver are making the Great Marsh their home again—some after an absence of a hundred years.

Student Conservation Association members help build an overlook along the new Great Marsh trail. *NPS*

Students help restore wetlands by transplanting native species. *( facing) NPS*

269

*Both photos by NPS, Jeff Manuszak*

## Prescribed Fires

Prescribed fire is a reconized strategy of natural area restoration. Fires are occassionally conducted in Duneland, but only with specific humidity and wind velocity.

## John Merle Coulter Nature Preserve

Land stewardship is an important activity of the Shirley Heinze Land Trust. In the years since it was founded in 1981, the Trust has preserved 1,200 acres of natural lands from neglect or unnecessary development. The Heinze organization works hard to restore its properties when that is needed—and this restoration can take many forms.

For instance, the ninety-acre John Merle Coulter Nature Preserve abuts the National Lakeshore's Tolleston Dunes area, east of the Lake/Porter County Line Road between Routes 12 and 20. In the 1930s, this area was extensively sand mined, and yet it has reverted to good-quality sand prairie and black oak savanna with more than four hundred species of plants, including nineteen endangered species. The endangered Karner blue butterfly lives at this site, but the lupine (which it eats) has to be protected from the large number of deer in the area. Like many Trust properties, it was in poor shape when it was purchased. Trash and concrete had to be removed, and prescribed burns were needed to stabilize the savanna ecosystems.

The Coulter property is now a dedicated state nature preserve.

A field of blooming blazing stars at the restored Coulter Preserve. *(above)*

Some restoration activities are easier in the winter. With the leaves gone, it is easier to see the entire area. One has to wear gloves anyway. *(left)*

*Both photos by Ron Trigg*

271

## Duneland Misconceptions and Urban Legends

*Misconception: Glaciers made the sand dunes.*

Although the glaciers did grind lots of rock into sand, the dunes were made by the wind blowing the sand away from the lake.

*Misconception: "Lake Chicago" was an arm of the sea.*

The name "Lake Chicago" has always been confusing. What geologists used to call "Lake Chicago" was a freshwater lake formed when the glaciers receded.

*Misconception: Lake Chicago was a different lake than Lake Michigan.*

Lake Chicago was always the same lake as Lake Michigan. The different name was used to denote its earlier stages when the lake drained through the Illinois and Mississippi Rivers. To reduce the confusion, the old term has been replaced by "Glacial Lake Michigan."

*Misconception: Mount Baldy is the tallest dune along the Lake Michigan shoreline in Indiana.*

Mount Tom is the tallest. Mount Baldy's fame is that it's a wandering, or moving, dune.

*Misconception: Claude Allouez and Claude Dablon were the first European explorers in the Calumet Area.*

There is no evidence that any European explorers were in Illinois before Marquette and Jolliet in 1673 and no evidence that any were in Indiana before Marquette in 1675.

*Misconception: Bailly was not really the first European settler.*

Some tombstones from the early 1800s have been weathered so badly that is nearly impossible to know if their death dates precede Bailly's arrival. They may date from the 1810s or the 1840s. Careful reexamination was inconclusive. There are no other records that imply settlement before 1822.

*Misconception: Anders Chellberg helped start the Augsburg Lutheran Church.*

The Augsburg church in Porter was established in 1858, five years before the Chellbergs' arrival.

*Misconception: Chanute was the first man to fly a glider.*

Octave Chanute apparently never did fly himself. He did publish the first scientific review of aviation experiments, he did (at the Dunes) conduct the first scientific experiments of various gliders, he did design the first reasonably-stable flying machine, and he did visit and advise the Wright Brothers.

*Misconception: Alice Gray (Diana of the Dunes) was the daughter of a prominent physician.*

Her father was Ambrose Gray, a Chicago laborer who didn't have much money.

*Misconception: Miller was named for a man named John.*

Miller (actually Miller Station) was named for Samuel Miller, who had a son named John.

*Misconception: NIPSCO's Michigan City Generating Station is nuclear-powered.*

The Michigan City Generating Station is coal-powered. It does have a cooling tower similar to the ones used elsewhere at nuclear-powered plants.

*Misconception: Fish caught in Lake Michigan shouldn't be eaten by people.*

The state of Indiana publishes guidelines on *how much* fish one should eat. Too much may be unhealthy.

## Indiana Dunes National Lakeshore Statistics

The National Lakeshore today has fifteen miles of lake Michigan shoreline and 15,177 acres of land (including the 2,182 within Dunes State Park). Parklands are located in Lake, Porter, and LaPorte Counties and in fifteen cities and towns.

It is the closest national park to Chicago, Indianapolis, and Milwaukee. It is actually closer to Detroit than any of the national parks in Michigan.

It is the number-one outdoor recreation destination in Indiana, with approximately 60 percent of its 1.9 million annual visitors coming from outside the state. Visitors to the park spend $54.9 million dollars in Northwest Indiana and support 772 jobs for local citizens, who earn $13.4 million.

## Sites and Features

- Fifteen miles of Lake Michigan shoreline
- Bailly Homestead National Historic Landmark
- Beaches, dunes, forests, wetlands
- Chellberg Farm
- Little Calumet River/Salt Creek
- Paul Douglas Environmental Learning Center
- Mount Baldy
- Dunes Learning Center
- The Great Marsh
- West Beach bathhouse and picnic area
- Cowles Bog
- Century of Progress Homes
- Pinhook Bog
- Dunewood Campground
- Heron Rookery
- Portage Lakefront and Riverwalk

- Forty-five miles of hiking, bicycle, equestrian, and cross-country skiing trails
- 225 known archaeological sites from Indian, fur trade, and Swedish immigration periods
- 4 National Natural Landmarks
- 1 National Historic Landmark
- 2 National Trails

## Flora and Fauna

- 46 species of mammals
- 60 species of butterflies
- 18 species of amphibians
- 1,200 species of ferns and flowering plants
- 71 species of fish
- more than 600 species of fungi
- 350 species of birds (resident and migrating)
- 23 species of reptiles
- 28 species of orchids (more native orchid species than Hawaii)
- 30 percent of Indiana's listed rare, threatened, endangered, and special concern plant species

Ahrendt, William J. *A Swedish Heritage: History of Burstrom Chapel.* Unpublished brochure: Chesterton, Indiana. 1975.

Bair, Craig. Indiana Department of Natural Resources e-mail. Copy held at the Westchester Township History Museum. January 11, 1999.

Ball, Timothy H. *Lake County, Indiana, from 1834 to 1872.* J. W. Goodspeed: Chicago. 1873.

———. (ed.). *Lake County, Indiana, 1884: An Account of the Semi-Centennial Celebration of Lake County, September 3 and 4, with Historical Papers and Other Interesting Records Prepared for this Volume.* Lake County Star: Crown Point, Indiana. 1884.

———. *Northwestern Indiana From 1800 to 1900.* Donohue and Henneberry: Chicago. 1900.

*Beverly Shores Golden Jubilee.* Unpublished brochure: Beverly Shores, Indiana. 1983.

Bieber, C. L., and Smith, Ned M. *Industrial Sands of the Indiana Dunes.* Bulletin no 7. Indiana Geological Survey: Bloomington, Indiana. 1952.

Blake, Darus P. "Early days in Lake and Porter Counties" in Lake County Historical Association. *History of Lake County, Volume 10.* Calumet Press: Gary, Indiana. 1929.

Blachley, Willis S. "Geology of Lake and Porter Counties, Indiana." *22nd Annual Report of the Department of Geology and Natural Resources of Indiana.* Indianapolis. 1897.

Botts, Lee. *Origin of the Dunes Learning Center.* Unpublished manuscript. 2011.

Bowers, John O. *The Old Bailly Homestead.* Privately published: Gary, Indiana. 1922.

———. *Dream Cities of the Calumet.* Calumet Press: Gary, Indiana. 1929.

Brennan, George A. *The Wonders of the Dunes.* Bobbs-Merrill: Indianapolis. 1923.

Briggs, William A. "Items of Interest Concerning Some Early Towns in Porter County." Reprinted July, 1960, in Coambs, Norris D. (ed.). *Duneland Notes* (unpublished newsletter). Duneland Historical Society: Chesterton, Indiana. Circa 1930.

———. "Taverns, Our First Hotels in Early Porter County." Reprinted August, 1968, in Coambs, Norris D. (ed.). *Duneland Notes* (unpublished newsletter). Duneland Historical Society: Chesterton, Indiana. Circa 1930.

Brock, Kenneth J. *Birds of the Indiana Dunes.* 2nd edition. Shirley Heinze Environmental Fund: Michigan City, Indiana. 1997.

Brown, Steven E., and Thompson, Todd A. *Geologic Terrains of the Chicago 30 x 60 Minute Quadrangle in Indiana.* Indiana Geological Survey: Bloomington, Indiana. 1995.

Brown, Steven E., Bleuer, N. K., and Thompson, Todd A. *Geologic Terrain Map of the Southern Lake Michigan Rim, Indiana.* Indiana Geological Survey: Bloomington, Indiana. 1996.

Cannon, Thomas H., Loring, Hanibal H., and Robb, Charles J. (eds.). *History of the Lake and Calumet Region of Indiana Embracing the Counties of Lake, Porter and LaPorte.* Historians Association: Indianapolis. 1927.

Carr, Drusilla. In Lester, J. W. (December 24, 1921). *Mrs. Drusilla Carr Tells of Early Days at Miller Beach.* Typewritten manuscript held at the Gary Public Library. 1921.

Charlebois, Patrice. "Nonindigenous Threats Continue." *The Helm, Volume 13,* number 1, pp. 5–7. 1996.

Chrzastowski, Michael J., and Thompson, Todd A. "Late Wisconsinan and Holocene Coastal Evolution of the Southern Shore of Lake Michigan." *Quaternary Coasts of the United States:*

*Marine and Lacustrine Systems.* SEPM Special Publication Number 48, pp. 397–413. 1992.

Clemensen, A. *Evaluation of Historic Resources at Bailly Homestead.* Typewritten manuscript at the Indiana Dunes National Lakeshore, Porter, Indiana. 1975.

Clifford, Mary Louise, and Clifford, J. Candace. *Women Who Kept the Lights.* Cypress Communications: Williamsburg, Virginia. 1993.

Cohen, Ronald D., and McShane, Stephen G. *Moonlight in Duneland: The Illustrated Story of the Chicago South Shore and South Bend Railroad.* Indiana University Press: Bloomington, Indiana. 1998.

Cook, Sarah Gibbard. *Henry Chandler Cowles and Cowles Bog, Indiana: A Study in Historical Geography and the History of Ecology.* Reprinted in 1999 by the Field Museum, Chicago. 1980.

Cook, Sarah Gibbard, and Jackson, Robert S. *The Bailly Area of Porter County, Indiana: The Final Report of a Geo-historical Study Undertaken on Behalf of the Indiana Dunes National Lakeshore.* Robert Jackson & Associates: Evanston, Illinois. 1978.

Corliss, Carlton J. *Main Line of Mid-America.* Creative Age Press: New York. 1950.

Cottman, George S. *Indiana Dunes State Park: A History and Description.* Publication Number 97. The Department of Conservation, State of Indiana: Indianapolis. 1930.

Cowles, Henry Chandler. "The Ecological Relations of the Vegetation on the Sand Dunes of Lake Michigan." *Botanical Gazette, Volume 27*, pp. 95–117, 167–202, 281–302, 361–91. 1899.

Cressey, George B. *The Indiana Sand Dunes and Shore Line of the Lake Michigan Basin.* The Geographic Society of Chicago Bulletin Number 8. University of Chicago Press: Chicago. 1928.

Crouch, Tom D. *Octave Chanute.* Brochure prepared in cooperation with the National Park Service, Indiana Dunes National Lakeshore. United States Government Printing Office: Washington, D. C. 1992.

Dabbert, James R. *The Indiana Dunes Revealed: The Art of Frank V. Dudley.* University of Illinois Press. Urbana. 2006.

D'Alto, Nick. "On Wind's Wings: Octave Chanute and the Indiana Dunes." *Traces of Indiana and Midwestern History. Volume 15, number 2.* 2003.

Danckers, Ulrich, and Meredith, Jane. *A Compendium of the Early History of Chicago to the Year 1835 when the Indians Left.* Inland Press: Menomonee Falls, Wisconsin. 2000.

Daniels, E. D. *A Twentieth Century History and Biographical Record of LaPorte County Indiana.* The Lewis Publishing Company: Chicago. 1904.

Deale, Valentine B. *The History of the Potawatomi before 1722.* Notre Dame University: Notre Dame, Indiana. 1939.

DeNeal, Lisa. "Aetna Powder Plant Accident Debunked." *Gary Post-Tribune.* [No date].

Design Organization. www.designorg.com/portfolio/civic/portagepavilion/portagepav.asp. Accessed August 24, 2011.

Donnelly, Joseph P. *Jacques Marquette, S. J.: 1637–1675.* Loyola University Press: Chicago. 1968.

*Dune Acres 1923–1973.* Dune Acres, Indiana. 1973.

Eccles, William J. *The French in North America.* Michigan State University Press: East Lansing, Michigan. 1998.

Edmunds, R. David. *The Potawatomis: Keepers of the Fire.* University of Oklahoma Press: Norman, Oklahoma. 1978.

Edwards, Janet Zenke. *Diana of the Dunes: The True Story of Alice Gray.* History Press: Charleston. 2010.

Engel, J. Ronald. *Sacred Sands: The Struggle for Community in the Indiana Dunes.* Wesleyan University Press: Middletown, Connecticut. 1983.

Esarey, Logan. *A History of Indiana from its Exploration to 1850.* Hoosier Heritage Press: Indianapolis. 1970.

Franklin, Kay, and Norma Schaeffer. "Porter Beach Fishermen Served Perch Dinners to Thousands of Hungry Chicagoans." *Dunes Country Magazine,* Spring, 1983.

Gilbertson, Dana. *Chesterton Tribune:* chestertontribune.com/Environment/lakeshore_volunteer_angel_gochee.htm. Accessed August 2011.

*Good Fellow Club Youth Camp, Chesterton, Indiana: Historic Structures Report and Cultural Landscape Report.* Indiana Dunes National Lakeshore: Porter, Indiana. 2005.

Goodspeed, Weston A., and Blanchard, Charles. *The Counties of Porter and Lake.* F. A. Battery and Company: Chicago. 1882.

Gray, Ralph D. *Public Ports for Indiana: A History of the Indiana Port Commission.* Indiana Historical Bureau: Indianapolis. 1998.

*Great Marsh Restoration at Indiana Dunes National Lakeshore.* Indiana Dunes National Lakeshore. [No date].

Greenberg, Joel. *A Natural History of the Chicago Region.* University of Chicago Press: Chicago. 2002.

Gudas, Ray. "Beverly Shores Lithuanian Enclave in the Dunes." *Michigan City News-Dispatch.* [No date.]

Henderson, Sandy. "The Steel Company and the Butterfly." In *The Indiana Dunes Story: How Nature and People Made a Park.* 2nd edition. Shirley Heinze Environmental Fund: Michigan City, Indiana. 1997.

Hendry, Fay L. "National Register of Historic Places Inventory— Nomination: Bailly, Joseph, Homestead and Cemetery." National Park Service: Washington, D. C. 1977.

"Historians hear history of Beverly Shores." *Chesterton Tribune.* March 24, 2010. http://chestertontribune.com/Local%20History/historians_hear_history_of_bever.htm. Accessed July 2011.

Hopkins, Eva. *A Chronology of Burns Harbor.* Typewritten manuscript held at the Westchester Township History Museum.

———. *Duneland Chronology.* Typewritten manuscript held at the Westchester Township History Museum.

———. *Elmer Johnson's Home on Oak Hill Road.* Unpublished manuscript synthesized from the *Chesterton Tribune* articles of June 20, 1912, June 3, 1926, June 26, 1947, January 20, 1949, and July 6, 1950 and Johnson family genealogies.

Howat, William F. *A Standard History of Lake County, Indiana, and the Calumet Region.* Lewis Publishing Company: Chicago. 1915.

Howe, Frances. *The Story of a French Homestead in the Old Northwest.* Press of Nitschke Brothers: Columbus, Ohio. 1907.

Indiana Department of Natural Resources. *Early Peoples of Indiana.* Indiana Department of Natural Resources: Indianapolis. 1999.

Indiana Department of Natural Resources: Division of Historic Preservation and Archaeology. *Shipwrecks in Indiana: Underwater Archaeology in Lake Michigan* www.in.gov/dnr/historic/files/shipwreck.pdf. Downloaded July 24, 2011.

Indiana Dunes National Lakeshore. *Cultural Landscape Report: Chellberg Farm.* Porter, Indiana. 2000.

James, Rich. "RDA funding, Support Key to Reclamation, Development of Lake Michigan Shoreline." *Indiana Economic Digest.* http://indianaeconomicdigest.com/ Main.asp?SectionID=31&SubSectionID=73&ArticleID=53922. Accessed August 24, 2011.

Kaufmann, Kira E. *Background Literature Review for Submerged Cultural Resources Within Indiana's Territorial Waters of Lake Michigan.* Commonwealth Cultural Resources Group, Inc., Milwaukee, Wisconsin. June, 2011.

Kellar, J. H. *An Introduction to the Prehistory of Indiana.* 2nd edition. Indiana Historical Society: Indianapolis. 1983.

Kenton, Edna (ed). *Jesuit Relations and Allied Documents: Travels and Explorations of the Jesuit Missionaries in North America (1610–1791).* Vanguard Press: New York. 1954.

Kiehn, David. *Broncho Billy and the Essanay Film Company.* Farwell Books: Berkeley, California. 2003.

Knotts, A. F. "Indian Trails, Towns and Mounds in Lake County." In Lake County Historical Association, *History of Lake County, Volume 10.* Calumet Press: Gary, Indiana. 1929.

Koelz, Walter. *Fishing Industry in the Great Lakes.* Indiana Department of Commerce Bureau of Fisheries: Indianapolis. 1926.

Lane, James B. *City of the Century: A History of Gary, Indiana.* Indiana University Press: Bloomington, Indiana. 1978.

Lane, James B., and Cohen, Ronald D. *Gary: A Pictorial History.* Donning Company: Norfolk, Virginia. 1983.

Lange, Henry. "Just a Little Land Deal. . . ." In *Porter: Historic Past . . . Promising Future.* Privately published pamphlet. 1983.

Lester, J. W. *Mrs. Drusilla Carr Tells of Early Days at Miller Beach.* Typewritten manuscript held at the Gary Public Library. December 24, 1921.

———. "Pioneer Stories of the Calumet." *Indiana Magazine of History, Volume 18,* pp. 166–76. 1922.

———. (using his American Indian name of Ni-gan-quet). "Lake Indians visit the camp sites of their ancestors." In Lester, James W. (ed.), *Historical Records of the Lake County Old Settler and Historical Association of Lake County, Indiana.* Crown Point, Indiana. 1924.

Levette, G. M. "Report of Observations Made in the Counties of DeKalb, Steuben, LaGrange, Elkhart, Noble, St. Joseph and LaPorte." In Cox, E. T., *Fifth Annual Report of the Geological Survey of Indiana, Made During the Year 1873.* Sentinel Company: Indianapolis. 1874.

Lieber, Richard. *Annual Report.* Indiana Department of Conservation: Indianapolis. 1922.

"Lincoln's Funeral in Michigan City, Indiana." *Lincoln Lore,* number 1491. May 1962.

*Log Homes of the 1930s: A Celebration of the History of Dune Acres.* Unsigned pamphlet. 2000.

Marimen, Mark, Willis, James, and Taylor, Troy. *Weird Indiana: Your Travel Guide to the Hoosier State's Local Legends and Best Kept Secrets.* Sterling Publishing: New York. 2008.

Mather, Stephen T. *Report on the Proposed Sand Dunes National Park, Indiana.* United States Department of the Interior: Washington, D. C. 1917.

McLellan, David, and Warrick, Bill. *The Lake Shore & Michigan Southern Railway.* Transportation Trails: Polo, Illinois. 1989.

Meyer, Alfred H. "Toponomy in Sequent Occupance Geography, Calumet Region, Indiana-Illinois." *Proceedings of the Indiana Academy of Science, Volume 54,* pp. 142–59. 1945.

———. "Circulation and Settlement Patterns of the Calumet Region of Northwest Indiana and Northeast Illinois. The Second Stage of Occupance—Pioneer Settler and Subsistence Economy, 1830–1850." *Annals of the Association of American Geographers, Volume 46,* pp. 312–56. 1956.

Middleton, William D. *South Shore: The Last Interurban.* Revised 2nd edition. Indiana University Press: Bloomington, Indiana. 1999.

Miller, Martha. *The Chellberg Family/The Chellberg Farm.* Millar Publications: Chesterton, Indiana. 1982.

Moore, Powell A. *The Calumet Region: Indiana's Last Frontier.* Indiana Historical Bureau: Indianapolis. Reprinted in 1977 with an afterword by Lance Trusty. 1959.

Morrow, Jim. *Beverly Shores: A Suburban Dunes Resort. Images of America* series. Arcadia Publishing: Chicago. 2001.

Munger, Elizabeth M. *Michigan City's First Hundred Years.* Typewritten manuscript at the Michigan City Public Library. (Published in 1990 by the Michigan City Historical Society: Michigan City, Indiana.) 1969.

National Park Service. "Early Development: 1870s–1910s." http://www.nps.gov/indu/historyculture/early_development.htm. Accessed November 26, 2010.

Newman, James E., and Lane, James B. (eds.). "Concerned Citizens Against the Bailly Nuclear Site." *Steel Shavings, Volume 16.* 1988.

Noble, Dennis L. "The Old Life Saving Station at Michigan City, Indiana 1889–1914." *Indiana History Bulletin, Volume 51,* number 10, pp. 136–43. October 1974. Reprinted by the Michigan City Historical Society, 1989.

———. "The United States Life Saving Service in Indiana: A Predecessor of the United States Coast Guard." *Indiana Military History Journal, Volume 8,* number 3, pp. 11–19. October 1983. Reprinted by the Michigan City Historical Society, 1989.

"Origin of the Town." Trail Creek Home Page: *www.townoftrail creek.com/page2.html,* which credits the LaPorte County Historical Society, Mary Monahan, and Paul Nelson. Accessed April 2011.

Packard, Jasper. *History of LaPorte County, Indiana, and its Townships, Towns and Cities.* S. E. Taylor & Company, Steam Printers: LaPorte, Indiana. 1876.

Parkman, Francis. *LaSalle and the Discovery of the Great West.* Little, Brown and Company: Boston. 1905.

Patterson, Arthur E. "The Pottawatomie Trail of Lake County." In Old Settler and Historical Association of Lake County, *History of Lake County, Volume XI.* Lake County Star Press: Crown Point, Indiana. 1934.

Pearson, Esther. "The History of Miller." Reprinted November, 1970, in Coambs, Norris D. (ed.). *Duneland Notes* (unpublished newsletter). Duneland Historical Society: Chesterton, Indiana.

Peel, Sara J. "Biotic Community Response to Stream Daylighting, Dunes Creek, Indiana." Paper presented at the 16th National Nonpoint Source Monitoring Workshop, September 14–18, 2008, Columbus, Ohio. 2008.

Pierce, Bessie Louise. *A History of Chicago.* Alfred A. Knopf: New York. 1937.

Podruchny, Carolyn. *Making the Voyageur World: Travelers and Traders in the North American Fur Trade.* University of Nebraska Press: Lincoln, Nebraska. 2006.

*Porter on Parade: Being a Brief History of the Founding of Porter and a Record of its Citizens, Past and Present.* Porter Centennial, Inc.: Porter, Indiana. 1959.

*The Prairie Club: Chicago.* Undated brochure held at the Calumet Regional Archives, Indiana University Northwest.

Read, Charlotte J. "How Citizens Saved the Indiana Dunes." *Environmental Education Report.* March 1983.

Read, Herbert. *Saving the Dunes: A Battle Waged over Decades.* Typewritten manuscript available at the Calumet Regional Archives.

Reed, Earl H. *The Dune Country.* Hardscrabble Books: Berrien Springs, Michigan. 1916.

Rehor, John A. *The Nickel Plate History.* Kalmbach Publishing Company: Milwaukee, Wisconsin. 1965.

Remini, Robert V. *Daniel Webster: The Man and His Time.* W. W. Norton & Company: New York. 1997.

Reshkin, Mark. "The Natural Resources of the Calumet: A Region Apart." In McShane, Stephen G., *Sand and Steel: The Dilemma of Cohabitation in the Calumet Region.* Indiana University Northwest: Gary, Indiana. 1987.

Richards, Rick. "Indiana State Prison a Part of Michigan City History." *The Beacher Weekly Newspaper, Volume 26,* number 19. May 20, 2010.

Scharf, Albert F. *Indian Villages of Chicago and Cook County.* Manuscript held by the Chicago Historical Society. 1903.

Schaeffer, Norma, and Franklin, Kay. "Industry Versus Preservation." In *The Indiana Dunes Story.* Shirley Heinze Environmental Fund: Michigan City, Indiana. 1984. (Reprinted in 1997).

Schiemann, Olga Mae. "Roads across Old Baillytown." *Duneland Historical Society, Volume II.* 1952.

Schneider, Allan F., and Keller, Stanley J. *Geologic Map of the 10 x 20 Chicago Quadrangle, Indiana, Illinois, and Michigan, Showing Bedrock and Unconsolidated Materials.* Indiana Geological Survey: Bloomington, Indiana. 1970.

Schoon, Kenneth J. *Calumet Beginnings: Ancient Shorelines and Settlements at the South End of Lake Michigan.* Indiana University Press: Bloomington, Indiana. 2003.

Shirley Heinze Environmental Fund. *The Indiana Dunes Story: How Nature and People Made a Park.* Newcomb Printing Services: Michigan City, Indiana. 1984. (Reprinted in 1997).

Simons, Richard S., and Parker, Francis H. *Railroads of Indiana.* Indiana University Press: Bloomington, Indiana. 1997.

Slupski, Janice. "The Glory Days of the Dunes Highway." *Singing Sands, Volume 19*, number 4. 1999.

*South Shore Lines, Volume 6*, number 11. September 1931.

Spicer, Steve. www.spicerweb.org/Miller/MillerHistory/carr.aspx. Accessed February 2011.

———. www.spicerweb.org/Miller/MillerHistory/explosionatthe powderworks.aspx. Accessed January 2011.

———. "Chanute's Diary. Monday, June 29, 1896." www.spicerweb .org/chanute/diary.aspx. Accessed December 2010.

*Splash Down Dunes Water Park.* Undated brochure.

Stodola, Barbara. *Michigan City Beach Communities. Images of America* series. Arcadia Publishing: Chicago. 2003.

Strong, A. D. "Magic Leaves the Enchanted Forest." *Gary Post-Tribune.* October 20, 1991.

Sullivan, Jerry. *Chicago Wilderness: An Atlas of Biodiversity.* Chicago Region Biodiversity Council: Chicago. [No date].

Svengalis, Kendall F. *Gary, Indiana: A Centennial Celebration.* Duneland Press: Westerly, Rhode Island. 2006.

Swenson, John F. "Jean Baptiste Point de Sable: The Founder of Modern Chicago." In Danckers, Ulrich, and Meredith, Jane, *A Compendium of the Early History of Chicago to the Year 1835 when the Indians Left.* Inland Press: Menomonee Falls, Wisconsin. 2000.

Tanner, Helen Hornbeck. *Atlas of Great Lakes Indian History.* University of Oklahoma Press: Norman, Oklahoma. 1987.

Thomas, Joseph (ed.). *A History of Ogden Dunes.* Ad-Craft Printers: Gary, Indiana. 1976.

Thompson, Ruth. *The Chapel of the Dunes 50th Anniversary.* Privately published: Gary, Indiana. 1951.

Thompson, Todd A. "Beach-Ridge Development and Lake-Level Bariation in Southern Lake Michigan." *Sedimentary Geology, Volume 80*, pp. 305–18. 1992.

Thwaites, Reuben Gold (ed.). "Voyages of Marquette." University Microfilms, Inc.: Ann Arbor, Michigan. A reprint of *Travels and Explorations of the Jesuit Missionaries in New France: 1610–1791, Volume LIX.* 1900. Burrows Brothers Company: Cleveland, Ohio. 1966.

Tinkham, Charles. "Diana of the Dunes." In JoAnne M. Grant and Marcia Carle (eds.), *The Dunes: Transformation as Inspiration.* Northern Indiana Arts Association: Munster, Indiana. 1986.

Trostel, Scott C. *The Lincoln Funeral Train: The Final Journey and National Funeral for Abraham Lincoln.* Cam-Tech Publishing: Fletcher, Ohio. 2002.

Troy, Silvia. "Citizen Action for Preservation." In *The Indiana Dunes Story: How Nature and People Made a Park.* 2nd edition. Shirley Heinze Environmental Fund: Michigan City, Indiana. 1997.

United States Bureau of the Census. *Census Returns for Lake, Porter and LaPorte Counties, Indiana.*

United States Coast Guard. www.uscg.mil/d9/sectlakemichigan/ STAMichiganCity.asp. Accessed May 2011.

Waldron, Larry. *The Indiana Dunes.* Eastern National: Fort Washington, Pennsylvania. 1998.

Warrick, Bill. *The Lincoln Funeral Train.* Herron Rail Video: Tampa, Florida.

———. *The Ogden Dunes Story.* Mid-American Heritage Preservation Foundation, Inc.: Whiting, Indiana. 2008.

Works Projects Administration. *The Calumet Region Historical Guide.* Garman Printing Company: Gary, Indiana. 1939.

Youngman, Peter. "Old Trails of Ogden Dunes and Vicinity." *Hour Glass, Volume 5*, number 10. Historical Society of Ogden Dunes: Ogden Dunes, Indiana. October 1997.

This photograph of the Chicago skyline taken by Tom Dogan from a boat near Michigan City clearly shows how the curvature of the earth causes the horizon to hide Chicago's street level as well as the lower portion of Chicago's tall buildings. *Tom Dogan*

Page numbers in *italics* represent illustrations.

KEN SCHOON, a Northwest Indiana native, is professor emeritus of science education at Indiana University Northwest. Dr. Schoon's research interests center around science misconceptions and local studies. Previous works include *Calumet Beginnings* and *City Trees,* a tree identification book. He is a board member and past president of the Dunes Learning Center and a member of the IU Northwest Science Olympiad committee.

On the Trail 8 trailhead boardwalk near the Wilson Shelter
at Indiana Dunes State Park. *M. A. Griswold, M.S.*

EDITOR: *Linda Oblack* · PROJECT EDITOR: *Darja Malcolm-Clarke* · COVER & INTERIOR DESIGNER: *Pamela Rude*

ASSISTANT EDITOR: *Sarah Jacobi* · PRINTER: *Four Colour Imports*